TRIUMPHBOOKS**.COM**

If These
WALLS
Could TALK:
GREEN BAY PACKERS

If These WALLS *Could* TALK:
GREEN BAY PACKERS

Stories from the
Green Bay Packers Sideline,
Locker Room, and Press Box

Wayne Larrivee with Rob Reischel

TRIUMPH
BOOKS

Copyright © 2016 by Wayne Larrivee and Rob Reischel

No part of this publication may be reproduced, stored in a retrieval system, or transmitted in any form by any means, electronic, mechanical, photocopying, or otherwise, without the prior written permission of the publisher, Triumph Books LLC, 814 North Franklin Street, Chicago, Illinois 60610.

Library of Congress Cataloging-in-Publication Data
Names: Larrivee, Wayne, author. | Reischel, Rob, 1969- author.
Title: If these walls could talk : Green Bay Packers : stories from the Green Bay Packers sideline, locker room, and press box / Wayne Larrivee and Rob Reischel.
Description: Chicago, Illinois : Triumph Books LLC, [2016]
Identifiers: LCCN 2016033968 | ISBN 9781629372792
Subjects: LCSH: Green Bay Packers (Football team)—Anecdotes. | Green Bay Packers (Football team)—History.
Classification: LCC GV956.G7 L37 2016 | DDC 796.332/640977561—dc23 LC record available at https://lccn.loc.gov/2016033968

This book is available in quantity at special discounts for your group or organization. For further information, contact:

Triumph Books LLC
814 North Franklin Street
Chicago, Illinois 60610
(312) 337–0747
www.triumphbooks.com

Printed in U.S.A.

ISBN: 978-1-62937-279-2

Design by Amy Carter

Photos courtesy of AP Images unless otherwise indicated.

*In the course of covering a pro football team, one works weekends
and holidays because that is when the games are played. Weekends
and holidays are "family time" for most people. I missed a lot of those
times over the years covering NFL football, but my wife, Julie,
and sons, Scott and Bryan, were extremely understanding and
accommodating. I can't thank them enough.*

—Wayne Larrivee

*To my children, Madison and Mia—your growth provides me
with pride and joy each and every day.*

—Rob Reischel

CONTENTS

CONTENTS

PROLOGUE

Why Green Bay?

The Packers were one of the two teams I loved as a kid. The other one was the New York Yankees.

I grew up in Lee, Massachusetts, in the 1960s, and the Yankees and Packers were my teams. I became particularly enamored with the Packers during the Lombardi years, thanks in part to the Ice Bowl and Jerry Kramer's book *Instant Replay*, which detailed the historic 1967 season.

I always thought it would be pretty cool to broadcast games for a team that I followed as a kid, so I had that in the back of my mind. If you are going to do NFL football on the radio every Sunday, what better place to do it than Lambeau Field? That was always my thought. It still is.

I'll never forget this: my first NFL broadcast as a Kansas City Chiefs announcer was in 1978. It was a preseason game at Lambeau Field in Green Bay. And it was the old Lambeau Field. The Pabst scoreboards were the only scoreboards—one on the north end, one on the south end.

It was a thrill to be there. Every time I work with James Lofton today, I remind him that 1978 was his rookie year with the Packers and I called his first game, which was also my first NFL game. Here I was in Green Bay, this place I had heard so much about but had never seen. My eyes were just dilated.

Green Bay was always my destination job. So when Jim Irwin announced his retirement following the 1998 season, I inquired about the position. I had a job broadcasting the Chicago Bears back then, so my inquiry was done very quietly. Many people in the business were telling me, "You don't want to do that."

By 1998, the Packers were good—winning division titles, making the playoffs, playing in two Super Bowls and winning one. Still, people were asking me, "Why would you want to do that? Why would you leave Chicago to go there?"

I'd say, "Well, it's not a business decision. It's one of those things that you just feel like you have to do." I said to myself, *You've been telling yourself and everybody that matters that this is what you'd like to do for a long time now.* If I didn't try and do it at that point, I knew I would go to my grave thinking, *You should have done that.*

So I did. I inquired about the Packers opening at WTMJ radio. And I'll never forget what happened after. I was doing the Chicago Cubs at the time, as well. I was filling in for Harry Caray, and we had a series in Milwaukee. While I was in town, I met with Jon Schweitzer, the general manager at WTMJ; Rick Belcher, who was the program director; and Paul LeSage, who ran the radio network.

So we met at Turner's, right across the street from the Bradley Center. We were having lunch, and at one point Jon said, "So you're doing the Bears, you're doing the Bulls, and you're doing the Cubs. Why do you want to come here?" And he kind of looked at me incredulously like, *What's wrong with you?* But I explained why I felt I wanted and needed to broadcast Packers football.

So we broke up and Jon and Rick headed off. LeSage and I were standing in front of the restaurant, and I was waiting for a cab. LeSage said to me, "I have someone in mind I would like to hire, but he's tied up with a national job." And I thought, *Well, that lunch interview went really well, didn't it? How about that?*

So this process went along during the entire 1998 season. Jim and Max (McGee) were leaving. They needed someone to pair with Larry McCarren, and they were looking at a bunch of candidates. It kind of went back and forth, and Jon called one day in late October and asked if we could meet. And I said, "Listen. Where is this going? Because if it's not going anywhere let's not even meet." But he said, "Yeah, it's going somewhere." So we met at a McDonald's on Interstate 94 at the Lake Forest Oasis and talked about the job. That meeting actually went well, and I really enjoyed visiting with Jon.

Weeks later, after being offered the job, I was starting to struggle with the decision. I knew that this move just didn't make any sense professionally. I was doing all this stuff in Chicago, I was in a market that appreciated me, and even the media people were great friends of mine. It was a wonderful situation.

At the station I was working for, WMAQ, the station manager, Wheezie Kramer, and program director, Lorna Gladstone (whom I had worked with at WGN), were really good to me. So were the Bears. Team president Mike McCaskey brought me into his office and promised that if the games changed stations, I would be protected, just as I was when they moved from WGN to WMAQ.

All of those years I thought if someone ever offered me the Packers job, it would be a slam dunk. I'd take it right on the spot. But there were a lot more factors involved. Everyone was really trying to get me to stay. The station and the team had really stepped up to the plate and let me know I was wanted. I was talking to myself a lot in those days, and I said, "I don't know if I can do this."

I talked it over with my wife, Julie, and sons, Scott and Bryan. At one point Scott said, "Dad, you always tell us to follow our dreams. If you don't do this, you're not following your dream." Maybe that was something I needed to hear.

That conversation, and the relationship I had started to build with Jon Schweitzer, ended up being the keys to convincing me to take the job. As I mentioned, I was working for terrific people in Chicago, but I felt very comfortable with Jon. I really wanted to work for him. He is just such a terrific person.

So in the end I just couldn't say no to my family, who knew this was what I had always hoped to do, or to Jon, who had gone through a long process himself to get to that point. Those people helped convince me in the end that this was what I had to do.

After the announcement, I got a lot of blowback from Chicago people. I still do today. I did not realize my impact in that market and that it would matter to people if I left, because I don't think in those terms. I didn't realize until I was halfway to Kenosha that there was somewhat of an uproar, and I thought, *Really? I'm just a play-by-play guy who left for another job. What's the big deal?*

Chicago is the greatest sports town in America. The fans make it the greatest. Chicago people follow their media almost as much as they love their players. They know a lot about the writers and the broadcasters, and it all becomes very personal with Chicago sports fans. That's different from every market that I've been in. Very different.

In the end, though, I made the move and it's been great. My son Scott went to the University of Wisconsin–Madison and met his future wife, Rachel Allen, while working for the late Marc Marotta at DOA. My younger son, Bryan, became my spotter working in the booth on Packers games for a decade. When I first brought Bryan in the Packers radio booth, some thought I was looking for a father-son bonding experience. That was not my original intent, but became a nice fringe benefit. Bryan was very professional and did an outstanding job of spotting the games. Within a few weeks, everyone understood and respected his important role on our broadcast team. He too went to UW–Madison and now works in Los Angeles. Our family has enjoyed Wisconsin. And for me, my childhood dream came true when I got to call the play-by-play for the Packers in Super Bowl XLV.

CHAPTER 1
HOW DID WE GET HERE?

Ｈow did we get here? Why was there consternation in Packer Nation over Green Bay's 2015 season? It was a year in which the Packers went 10–6 in the regular season and won a road playoff game, before losing an overtime thriller in Arizona in the NFC Divisional playoffs.

There was a time when this type of season was reason for celebration in Packers Nation—1989 certainly comes to mind.

Following an overtime loss to Seattle in the NFC Championship Game in January 2015, expectations were high for the 2015 Packers. It was a "Super Bowl or bust" mentality, and no one shied away from that goal.

Green Bay began the year 6–0, then struggled down the stretch, losing six of its final 10 games. The Packers also had their four-year run of NFC North Division championships snapped when Minnesota won at Lambeau Field in the regular season finale.

To listen to the passionate fan base, it almost seemed as if these Packers had a losing season. But the 2015 Packers—or, as coach Mike McCarthy called them, the 95th Green Bay Packers—won 10 games, made the postseason, and won a playoff game! How bad is that?

However, we in Packerland now live in a world where expectations are not only unprecedented in the history of this franchise, but at one time would have been unimaginable. Believe me, this is a good thing, because for many people my age who lived through a quarter century of Green Bay Packers football after Vince Lombardi, a mere nonlosing season was cause for celebration.

Prior to 1992, this beloved franchise had periods of championship success, but nothing quite like the sustained success it has enjoyed since the revival of Titletown.

In their first eleven years in the NFL, the Curly Lambeau Packers never posted a losing record. They also never finished higher than third in the league.

Starting in 1929 and continuing through 1944, the Packers won six

NFL Championships, becoming the first legitimate dynasty in NFL history.

But from 1945 through 1958 the Packers managed just three winning seasons, two 6–6 campaigns, and nine losing years. After a 2–10 record in 1949, the Packers parted ways with Lambeau—their founder and only coach—but their fortunes failed to improve.

Over the next nine years, the best the Packers could manage under coaches Gene Ronzani, Lisle Blackbourn, and Ray "Scooter" McLean were two 6–6 seasons. Are you starting to see a pattern here? The Packers would have periods of success, and then long stretches of futility. Perhaps it was the market in which they played, but that's an issue for later.

Following a 1–10–1 season in 1958, the Packers hired Lombardi, who had been an assistant coach with the New York Giants. Lombardi took command of this franchise, ruling with an iron fist. First, he reduced the influence of the Executive Committee on the football operations; then, he took the franchise to new heights.

In Lombardi's initial meeting with quarterbacks and other offensive players, he made his expectations known.

"He told us, 'I am not remotely interested in being just good,'" quarterback Bart Starr explained. "We are going to relentlessly chase perfection, knowing full well that we won't catch it, because nobody is perfect. But in the process, we'll catch excellence."

Those words resonated in Starr's mind.

"I almost jumped out of my chair, I was so excited," Starr said.

When the meeting ended, Starr raced out of the room to use a phone—the rotary variety—to call his wife, Cherry.

"I told her, 'Honey, we're going to begin to win,'" Starr said. "I couldn't wait to get going."

It just so happened that color television was coming to life at that time, and the Packers became a national team. Between 1961 and 1967, Green Bay won five championships, including the first two Super Bowls.

Starr, Ray Nitschke, Paul Hornung, Jerry Kramer, and many others became household names at that time. They captured the nation's attention, and developed a whole new generation of young fans.

I know I was one of them, growing up in a small town in western Massachusetts. The Packers became "America's Team" before the Dallas Cowboys took that moniker in the 1970s. The 1967 NFL Championship game known as the Ice Bowl became legendary, and Lambeau Field became a historic football Mecca.

Prior to the Ice Bowl, the Packers won their first championship under Lombardi by blowing out the New York Giants 37–0 in the 1961 title game.

In 1965, Don Chandler's questionable game-tying field goal in the fog tied the Western Conference playoff game against the Baltimore Colts and the Packers went on to win 13–10 in overtime at Lambeau. The following week, Paul Hornung and Jim Taylor ran over the defending champion Cleveland Browns 23–12, while the Ray Nitschke–led defense held Jim Brown to 50 rushing yards in what was the future Hall of Fame running back's last game.

It can be argued that game made Nitschke a Hall of Fame Player because he was such a dominant force on a snowy and slick Lambeau Field. By the end of the 1960s, some of the NFL's greatest moments had taken place on that 100-yard field laid out between Ridge Avenue and Oneida Street in tiny Green Bay, Wisconsin, of all places.

After the iconic Lombardi left, history repeated itself in Green Bay. From 1968 through 1991, the Packers had just four winning seasons and two postseason appearances in 24 years.

The Packers won just one playoff game during that period. And by the dawn of unfettered NFL free agency in 1993, there was a strong belief a team in a small northern market like Green Bay would never win again. The masses all wondered, *What free agent would go to the league's northernmost outpost out of his own "free agent" will?*

CHAPTER 2
TITLETOWN TURNAROUND

In 1989, I was still working in Chicago at WGN as the Bears' play-by play announcer. I had a conversation with Bryan Harlan, the team's associate public relations director.

The Packers were looking for a president and CEO. And Bob Harlan—Bryan's dad—was the prime candidate.

Bryan told me that if the club did not name his dad—who had worked in several roles with the team since 1971—to the lead post, he would probably leave the organization.

Years later, Bob told me, "I wasn't going to leave the organization if I didn't get the job. Part of the holdup was the fact no one outside of Green Bay had ever held that position."

Well, the Packers' Executive board got it right. Bob Harlan was named president and CEO and the first building block in the Titletown revival story was in place.

"We had to change the way we were doing things because it wasn't working," Harlan said. "In 24 years we had seen just two postseasons, only four winning seasons, and one playoff victory."

Two years into his tenure, Harlan's first significant move was to fire general manager Tom Braatz and hire Ron Wolf, a longtime scout with Oakland and the New York Jets, as Green Bay's general manager. Harlan gave Wolf full authority over the football operations with no interference.

Harlan separated the organization into two components: business and football. It was up to the business side to provide the financial resources for the football side to win.

With the second building block in place, Wolf fired head coach Lindy Infante after the 1991 season and hired San Francisco 49ers offensive coordinator Mike Holmgren as head coach. Holmgren was a noted "quarterback whisperer," and Wolf undoubtedly had that in mind when he traded a first-round draft pick to Atlanta for someone named Brett Favre, a 1991 second-round selection by the Falcons.

Wolf first fell in love with Favre while working as the New York Jets' personnel director. Wolf was preparing for the 1991 draft, and both he and Jets general manager Dick Steinberg agreed that Favre was the No. 1 player in that year's draft.

The Jets didn't have a first-round draft choice that year. When Favre fell out of the first round, though, the Jets tried trading up ahead of Atlanta—which was known to covet Favre.

Steinberg thought he had a deal worked out with Phoenix, one slot ahead of Atlanta. But the Cardinals pulled out at the last moment, and the Falcons took Favre with the 33rd overall pick.

That move was a blow to the Jets, who selected quarterback Browning Nagle—an all-time bust—one pick later. Then–Jets coach Bruce Coslet lobbied hard for Nagle, and Steinberg eventually made Nagle his pick.

In the end, that was a huge break for Wolf and the Packers.

"From my standpoint, in the long run, it worked out perfectly for me," Wolf said. "If Brett wasn't in Atlanta, he would have been in New York and I wouldn't have been able to get him.

"I think certainly in his era he'd be in the top five [players]. When you think of somebody now, you think of the great tradition…that great tradition of the Green Bay Packers. So for Brett Favre to be now said to be the greatest player ever to play for the Green Bay Packers, that's rare air, rarefied air."

Now there were four building blocks in place—Harlan, Wolf, Holmgren, and Favre. But arguably the biggest piece of the puzzle was yet to come.

A new era of the NFL had begun. In 1993, for the first time in league history, unfettered free agency was beginning. This was considered a death knell for the small-market franchises, especially those "up north" like Green Bay and Buffalo.

But it was little Green Bay that landed the biggest free agent perhaps of all time when future Hall of Fame defensive end Reggie White left

Philadelphia for Green Bay. The Packers outbid the San Francisco 49ers, among other major market powers, for White's services.

A deeply religious man—an ordained minister, the "Minister of Defense"—Reggie used to joke that he came to Green Bay because "God told [him] to come here." In reality, he came to the Packers because he believed Brett Favre was a Super Bowl–caliber quarterback, and what White wanted more than anything was a quarterback and a team that could win a championship. That judgment—and $17 million over four years—made the difference.

"That's what changed the football fortunes of this franchise. It was huge," Harlan said of signing White. "Everyone thought the last place he would sign was Green Bay, and it was monumental because not only did he sign, but he recruited for Green Bay and got guys [such as] Sean Jones to come here. He sent a message to the rest of the NFL that Green Bay was a great place to play."

White's signing put the final building block in place for the Titletown revival. But even bigger than that, his signing sent a message to the rest of the NFL that free agents—yes, even African American free agents—could go to Green Bay and thrive. That is a message that resonates to this day.

The Packers' Fab Five—Harlan, Wolf, Holmgren, Favre, and White—were the principals in reviving a historic but moribund franchise. In my opinion, the turnaround wouldn't have happened if even one of this quintet wound up elsewhere.

To me, the most important block was Harlan. Without him, the rest of puzzle pieces don't fall neatly into place.

This group made the Packers relevant for the first time in nearly a quarter of a century. And since 1992, the Packers have had almost 25 years of sustained success with three Super Bowl appearances, two Super Bowl wins, and 17 playoff appearances—including seven straight trips to the postseason.

I know this sounds crazy to Packers fans under the age of 25, but had those five men not come together, who knows what would have become of the Packers in today's NFL.

From Wolf to Mike Sherman to Ted Thompson; from Holmgren to Ray Rhodes, Mike Sherman, and Mike McCarthy; and from Favre to Aaron Rodgers, today's expectations are perhaps higher than any time in franchise history.

Playoff appearances and division titles aren't good enough anymore. It's "Super Bowl or bust" on an annual basis.

As Mike McCarthy said at his first press conference after being named Green Bay's head coach in January 2006, "We're gonna bring a world championship here to Green Bay. That's the goal, the expectation."

That expectation was met in 2010, when McCarthy's Packers hoisted the Lombardi Trophy. And Green Bay has been in the Super Bowl picture ever since.

That's why 10–6 can feel like 6–10, and just two playoff games in a single season is a disappointment to the fan base. That's why you heard and felt so much consternation from Packers Nation about the 2015 season.

Blame that Fab Five. They revived this franchise to an incredibly high level of sustained success. They raised the bar, and that's how we got here.

CHAPTER 3
RAY RHODES

The choice of Ray Rhodes as the Green Bay Packers' 12th head coach stunned much of the NFL. Twelve months later, following an 8–8 season, Packers general manager Ron Wolf made an even bolder move and fired Rhodes just one year into a four-year contract.

Therefore, Rhodes joined Ray "Scooter" McLean in 1958 as the only head coaches in Packer history to last just one season.

"Our players did not respond to this program," Wolf said the day he dismissed Rhodes. "It's not good enough with the team that we have. It's not acceptable."

The Packers had become one of the NFL's elite teams during Mike Holmgren's seven-year tenure (1992–98). They won 67 percent of their games during that time, won the 31st Super Bowl, and lost the 32nd Super Bowl.

When Holmgren left for Seattle after the 1998 season, Wolf made the surprising move of picking Rhodes.

Rhodes had been Green Bay's defensive coordinator for two years under Holmgren, and then was Philadelphia's head coach from 1995 to 1998. Rhodes went 29–34–1 with the Eagles, and was fired following a 3–13 season in '98.

"The seat is going to be hot," said Rhodes, who became the first African American coach in Packers history. "The shoes are going to be big to fill.

"The key is to keep the machine running, keep the machine going. Make sure if you need a new tire here, or a new tire there, you put it on. But don't mess with the engine. Don't mess with it."

But the Packers often performed like a broken-down jalopy under Rhodes. Part of that was due to a lack of discipline under Rhodes. Part of it was a roster than had started to decline.

I remember the expectations in 1999 were really high. The Packers had just lost a wild-card playoff game to San Francisco at the end of the 1998 season, and were still considered one of the best teams in football.

I remember watching Antonio Freeman my first summer in Green

Bay. He had dominated the league at wide receiver for three straight seasons. He was the best receiver in the NFL, but he was holding out. Finally, halfway through camp, Ron Wolf signed him. Well, Freeman came in, and I was watching practice and not seeing the guy I saw dominate the league. And I said something to Larry McCarren about that.

Ray Rhodes said to me, "Do you see the free agents jumping line?" I said, "What do you mean?" He said, "They're all jumping line to get opposite Freeman because they can cover him." All the rookie free agents, all the defensive backs were trying to line up opposite Freeman. He was right. He couldn't run anymore. He went from the Pro Bowl in February to a guy where free agents just couldn't wait to cover him in practice by August. And he was never the same again. He was never that dominant. He was a good receiver, but that was about it. And the Packers were paying him to be the best receiver in the league.

So to me, that's where everything started. And it was all downhill from there. And I kept thinking during training camp that this did not look like a Super Bowl team. Now, I'm just a layman, but it sure didn't look like a team that could be special, and they never really were.

They had all of those veterans still around from those back-to-back Super Bowls, but the window in the NFL closes so fast. And they had a roster that was starting to age. Green Bay's draft classes also weren't producing like they did earlier in Ron Wolf's tenure.

Green Bay won three of its first four games that year, but needed dramatics from Brett Favre to do so each time. I'll never forget that first game against the Raiders, with the back-and-forth and, finally, the dramatic win at the end. Favre hit tight end Jeff Thomason with a one-yard touchdown with just 11 seconds left to give the Packers a 28–24 win. My oldest son Scott had just enrolled at the University of Wisconsin–Madison, and he was there for that game. We were coming down the elevator from the press box after the game and Scott turned to me and said, "Well, Dad, this is what we came here for."

The Packers then dropped four of five and fell to 4–5 on the season. A three-game winning streak briefly restored hope before the Packers dropped three straight. The 8–8 record was Green Bay's worst since the 4–12 campaign in 1991. That led to Green Bay missing the playoffs for the first time since 1992.

The Packers' dominance of the 1990s was officially over as they ended the decade with a disappointing season.

"I make no excuses," Rhodes said after he was fired. "This is a business about getting things done, and I understand that. This was a tough year for a lot of our guys."

It wasn't just the win-loss record that prompted Wolf to make a coaching change. It was also a lack of discipline, fire, and intensity.

After seven years of Holmgren's no-nonsense, dictatorial approach, Rhodes elected to loosen the reins with a veteran team. Unfortunately for Rhodes, that approach did not work.

Many of the veterans still needed to be coached hard, and took advantage of the softer standards. Several of the team's younger players also made costly mistakes, for which there didn't appear to be any repercussions.

Wolf also didn't sense any passion when he watched his team practice, and later referred to the atmosphere as a "country club."

"You can get a pretty good pulse of the team at practice," Wolf said. "There was a different pulse in the latter part of the season. I think that reflected in our play."

Not everyone was happy with Wolf's decision to pull the plug on Rhodes after just one year.

"I was pretty upset after he was fired after just one year," Packers Pro Bowl safety LeRoy Butler said. "Not necessarily at Ron, but more the process. I mean, we were spoiled at the time, and 8–8 wasn't good enough. But when you look at that roster we had [in 1999], Ray needed more than one year. So I appreciated him getting a shot, but he should have gotten at least three years.

Despite having one of football's top players in Brett Favre (right), Ray Rhodes and the Packers went just 8–8 during a disappointing 1999 season.

"With Holmgren, they would police you. But with Ray Rhodes, you would police yourself. Every guy holds another guy accountable. So it's hard to tell a grown man to be in by 9 o'clock, and guys took advantage of it."

Rhodes, who had a reputation as a defensive guru, couldn't get that side of the ball fixed, and the Packers allowed their most points since 1990. In the end, it all added up to a fantastically frustrating year for all involved.

"You would hope Ray would get a better chance to get his system in place, but I think Ron thought we were too friendly with Ray," Butler said. "And maybe some of us were. With as many young players as we had, you need discipline. We didn't always have that."

Overall, I thought Ray Rhodes was just a great guy. He was terrific to work with. He really was. I know they hired him to be a disciplinarian. I don't think that he ever was. And when Ron fired Ray, he said he made a mistake and misjudged who Ray really was. But it wasn't solely Rhodes' fault. The core of that team was aging, and they had lost their edge. The window of opportunity does not remain open indefinitely, and for the great Packers teams of the 1990s, it shut once and for all during that 1999 campaign.

They won a lot of close games early, largely on the heroics of Favre, but there's no doubt he missed Holmgren. They all missed Holmgren and Holmgren's drive. And Ron Wolf just miscalculated on that hire. But I give Wolf all the credit in the world because if he did something wrong, he didn't stick with it. He wasn't worried about what the press was going to say or the people might say. He just went and made the change, and he was not going to live with that mistake. And that was what made him a Hall of Fame general manager.

And that's how I kind of look at that. Ron made a mistake and he knew it, and he corrected it right away. It was time to move on. I think when Holmgren left, Brett lost his mentor and his compass. Sherman Lewis was the offensive coordinator, and he was not an authoritative type at all. I liked Sherm a lot, and he was very helpful to me. But he was not the kind of guy who would coach Brett hard. And Brett needed to be coached hard.

Brett's dad coached him hard. Holmgren coached him hard. I think even in 2006 and 2007, Mike McCarthy coached him hard. McCarthy wouldn't allow him to fire his rocket balls, and all that stuff. That's one reason they turned it around so quickly under McCarthy. But I think they really missed Holmgren, both on and off the field. Plus, Holmgren took a significant portion of that front office with him as well.

That was an interesting time. That was an interesting year and a disappointing year. Unfortunately for Rhodes, it was over quickly in Green Bay.

CHAPTER 4
BRETT FAVRE

Brett Favre was simply one of the most charismatic performers in the legendary history of the Green Bay Packers, and really, the entire NFL.

Favre's route to Green Bay was somewhat circuitous, to say the least. On the first day of the 1991 NFL draft, the Philadelphia Eagles made a deal with the Packers to swap first-round draft choices. The Eagles moved into the Packers' position of No. 8 overall, and selected Tennessee offensive tackle Antone Davis. The Packers moved back to 19th in that round, but then–general manager Tom Braatz also acquired the Eagles' first-round pick in the 1992 draft.

Meanwhile, the Atlanta Falcons selected a talented but unpolished quarterback out of Southern Mississippi with the 33rd overall pick in 1991 named Brett Favre.

New York Jets personnel director Ron Wolf was especially disappointed, because Favre was going to be his selection with the 34th pick that year.

As Wolf was preparing for the 1991 draft, both he and Jets general manager Dick Steinberg agreed Favre was the No. 1 player on their board.

But Wolf and the Jets narrowly missed out of Favre when the Falcons selected him with the 33rd overall pick

Seven months later, the Packers were in the midst of a miserable 4–12 campaign. Then–Packers CEO Bob Harlan relieved Braatz of his duties and hired Wolf, giving him full control of the football operations.

Wolf was hired as Green Bay's general manager on November 27, 1991. And as fate would have it, the Packers were in Atlanta to play the Falcons four days later.

Wolf had kept close tabs on Favre throughout the 1991 season. And before the game, Wolf told Harlan he was going down to the field to scout Atlanta's backup quarterback.

Wolf said that if he liked what he saw, he was going to trade for that player. Just one thing: Harlan wasn't sure who the Falcons' backup quarterback was.

"Ron left and I started looking at the roster to see who the backup quarterback is," Harlan chuckled. "And Ron came back shortly before kickoff and said, 'Bob, we're going to make a trade for Brett Favre. Are you OK with that?' And I told him, 'I promised you it was your team to run and there would be no interference; I'm fine with it.' "

At the time, Favre's career statistics were 0-for-4 with two interceptions. Favre had fallen out of favor with Falcons coach Jerry Glanville due to his hard-partying lifestyle, and he'd plummeted to third string on Atlanta's depth chart.

Glanville wanted Favre out, and Wolf was happy to oblige.

"I had to get him out of Atlanta," Glanville said in a 2010 interview. "I could not sober him up. I sent him to a city where at 9:00 at night the only thing that's open is Chili John's. You can get it two ways, with or without onions. If I would have traded him to New York, nobody to this day would have known who Brett Favre ever was."

To this day, both Favre and Wolf disagree strongly with Glanville.

"I think he's covering his rear end. I mean, what a mistake, huh?" Wolf said. "I mean, you're talking about a first-ballot Hall of Famer. Every time you go out scouting, this is the one guy you look for. Someone you can hang your franchise on. And they had him in the building and they kept Billy Joe Tolliver over him. And no matter what you do or what you say you made a huge error there."

Added Favre: "I disagree with Jerry, because I think if I went somewhere else, where I knew I was going to be playing, I would have cared a lot more. Whether that was New York or Chicago, I just would have cared more. That's human nature."

When Wolf watched Favre throw that day in Atlanta, he saw a player whose arm strength matched anyone in football. He saw a player with remarkable upside. And Wolf knew Favre was his guy.

"We came back and at some point we had an executive committee meeting," Wolf said. "I told the people that we were going to make a commitment for this quarterback, told them all about this quarterback, Brett Favre, and how we were going to go work to get him. They had no idea who I was talking about. But they were all for it."

The following February, armed with two first-round draft picks, Wolf traded the first-round pick acquired by Braatz the previous year—the No. 17 overall selection—to Atlanta for Favre. Making the deal, though, wasn't easy.

Wolf and Falcons vice president of player personnel Ken Herock—one of his closest friends—talked four to five times a week for approximately 10 weeks.

Wolf offered a second-round draft pick for Favre. The Falcons demanded a No. 1.

Wolf said if he'd give them a first-rounder, he had to get something back. The Falcons balked.

"Finally the call came that said, 'It's got to be a first or we're not going to make the trade,'" Wolf said. "I knew that they wanted to get rid of him. It was just a matter of getting it done. I knew we were going to get this deal done because I didn't think anyone was going to pay what they were asking for other than me."

Wolf figured it didn't pay to play hardball any longer, and just 75 days into his tenure as Packers GM, he made the deal.

"I looked at it like this: if I was going to be successful, I was going to be successful because of Brett Favre," Wolf said. "And if he wasn't good enough, then I wasn't going to be successful. So I put everything on him and it worked out."

Favre was stunned when he first heard the news. Then he realized this could be the break he needed.

"There were a couple different ways I looked at it," Favre said. "Basically I went through the emotions. And first of all there was this initial shock that you were traded. Your first impulse is that's not a good thing.

"But the second thing is you're traded for a first-round pick, and that's basically better than being drafted in the first round because someone thinks highly enough of you to go through all this. So it was exciting for me.

"I felt like this was a great opportunity. I didn't know a whole lot about the Packers at the time. But I knew a lot about the history of the franchise in general, and I knew the franchise was struggling. So I knew this was an opportunity I was lucky to get."

Back then, few around the league even knew how to pronounce Favre's name! Well, we all learned quickly, as Favre changed everything in Green Bay, the NFC Central Division, and the entire NFL.

Favre was not anointed the starting quarterback right away in Green Bay. New head coach Mike Holmgren started veteran Don Majkowski— the "Majik Man"—at the outset of the 1992 season. But the oft-injured Majkowski suffered an ankle injury in the first quarter of a Week 3 game against Cincinnati in Green Bay.

Favre entered on just the Packers' second series, and he seemed lost at times.

"When I became a starter, I had no clue what was going on," Favre said. "Maybe that was good. If I told you back then I knew what was going on, I was feeding you a line of BS."

But Favre certainly appeared to know what he was doing by the end of that Bengals game.

Green Bay trailed 20–10 in the fourth quarter when Favre engineered an 88-yard touchdown drive. Favre capped the march with a five-yard touchdown to Sterling Sharpe, the first of 41 touchdowns on which that duo connected.

Then, with the Packers in a 23–17 hole in the final minute, Favre somehow led Green Bay on a 92-yard, game-winning march. The clincher came when Favre hit wideout Kitrick Taylor for a 35-yard touchdown with just 13 seconds left.

Amazingly, it was the only touchdown of Taylor's NFL career. And for Favre, it was the first of his 30 fourth-quarter comebacks and 45 career game-winning drives.

"It's probably a game that will be talked about forever," Favre said. "And a big reason for that is it's the one that kick-started everything, it's the one that got it going."

Favre went on to start an NFL quarterback–record 253 consecutive regular season games (275 including playoffs) while in Green Bay. He played 16 seasons for the Green and Gold and led them to two Super Bowls, winning one.

Favre won three straight MVP awards between 1995 and 1997. And Favre remains tied for the most regular season wins ever by an NFL quarterback (186).

The records and accomplishments are all well documented. But that's not why people became so enamored with Favre and the Packers during his 16-year run. It was the way he played the game that had everyone in the stadium on the edge of their seats.

People wonder about the lower bowl of Lambeau Field being bleacher seats without backs. With Favre and the Packers rolling, no one was sitting back in their seats anyways. Seat backs were not necessary!

"I've always told people he plays with a sandlot enthusiasm for the game, and you don't see that very often," Harlan said. "He was a fun-loving guy who played very well and showed delight in playing. Sometimes your fans say, 'I like college football because of the enthusiasm.' I think Brett put that same enthusiasm on the field on Sundays, and I thought that was enormous for the game."

Even in his first year as a starter, Favre gave everyone a portent of things to come.

The Cincinnati game that year was the first come-from-behind victory engineered by Favre. Another happened later that first season, and it wasn't just about winning a game.

Packer Nation loved Brett Favre's production during his 16 years in Green Bay. But Favre also endeared himself to the fan base with his unbridled love and childhood enthusiasm for the game.

Favre led a spirited comeback to beat the Philadelphia Eagles 27–24 in a mid-November game. Favre suffered a first-degree left shoulder separation that day, but played through the injury.

Favre's toughness certainly impressed Eagles defensive end Reggie White, who signed a free-agent contract in Green Bay that offseason and mentioned Favre as a major reason why.

White chose Green Bay largely because he believed their young quarterback could lead the Packers to the Super Bowl. The "Minister of Defense" wasn't wrong. And I don't think White comes to Green Bay without Favre on the roster.

In 1996, with Favre leading the offense and White spearheading the defense, Green Bay reached Super Bowl XXXI. It was the Packers' first trip to the Super Bowl in 29 years, and they made the most of it with a convincing 35–21 win over New England.

"The biggest thing I remember was holding that trophy up and seeing [Vince] Lombardi's name," Packers safety LeRoy Butler said. "It brought a tear to my eye because we said the trophy was coming back home. It was supposed to represent this city and these fans. They named the trophy after a former Green Bay Packer. I mean, it can't get any bigger than that."

Former Packers guard Aaron Taylor agreed.

"You can't replicate what it is we did," Taylor said. "That was an unbelievable team, an unbelievable time, an unbelievable experience."

Favre finished the 1996 season with 39 touchdown passes and just 13 interceptions despite operating with a depleted receiving corps. Favre's passer rating (95.8) was second to San Francisco's Steve Young's, and Favre ranked fourth in passing yards (3,899).

Favre won his second MVP Award that year, joining Don Hutson as the only other Packer at the time to win that honor twice.

"That was a pretty special year, a pretty special time," Favre said. "Great group of guys. We really were like family. And obviously things were pretty terrific on the field, as well. Those are the kinds of seasons you never forget."

My first in-person exposure to Favre came in 1992, while I was broadcasting Chicago Bears football. We were in Green Bay in Week 8, and Favre went 20-of-37 for 214 yards with one touchdown and one interception. He was also sacked four times that day as the Bears rolled to a 30–10 win.

Later that season, Favre and the Packers came to Chicago and toppled the Bears 17–3. Favre completed 16-of-24 passes that day for 209 yards with one touchdown and no interceptions.

Amazingly, Favre went 13–3 at Soldier Field during his Green Bay career. And over the last 24 years, the Packers are a remarkable 35–14 against Chicago—including a win at Soldier Field in the 2010 NFC Championship Game.

Favre's durability is the stuff of legend, especially when you consider most of his career was played at a time when the rules didn't protect quarterbacks to the level they do today.

Favre, who also played one year with the New York Jets and two in Minnesota, started an NFL-record 321 consecutive games (including playoffs). Of those, 275 starts came in Green Bay.

"I think that streak means more today than it ever has," Favre said. "I knew it was important. I knew it was tough to do week in and week out. It's so tough each week just to get yourself prepared mentally. That really is tough and can be a grind. But then the physical element is even harder.

"None of the things I accomplished are possible unless you're playing…for a long time. And to play all those years and to fight through a lot of things and keep going, I really have to tip my hat to myself on that one."

In addition to Favre's shoulder separation in the 1992 game against Philadelphia, Favre had a bevy of injuries that would have sidelined most mere mortals.

In 1995, Favre had a severely sprained left ankle and took just six snaps in practice that week. He then went and threw five touchdowns in a critical 35–28 win over Chicago.

Favre had the wind knocked out of him twice and coughed up blood in a 1995 game against Pittsburgh. But he stayed in the game and led the Packers to their first divisional title since 1972.

Favre suffered a sprained right thumb during the 1999 preseason, but played the entire season with the injury. Favre had a sprained lateral collateral ligament in his left knee in 2002. But he returned after a bye week and powered the Packers past Miami on *Monday Night Football*, despite playing with a brace on the knee.

Favre broke his right thumb on his throwing hand early in the 2003 season, and played with a splint for nearly three months. Still, Favre didn't miss a game.

"Here's a quarterback with a broken thumb that everybody's really taking for granted," Marco Rivera said of Favre late in that 2003 season. "And we expect him to go out there and have a Brett Favre kind of day. I don't know if I could even throw the ball with a broken thumb and he's doing it. He's unbelievable."

Favre said the broken thumb was the worst injury he ever had to deal with. Amazingly, one week after breaking his thumb in St. Louis, Favre threw three touchdowns and led the Packers to a rare win in Minnesota.

"I think the one game in my mind that comes up the most was the Minnesota game after I broke my thumb the previous week against St. Louis," Favre said. "To go and do that in a dome where we had no success in…that was pretty special.

"It was so hard to grip the ball and throw it like you want to. And then I went and played one of the best games of my life. That was pretty amazing. It felt a lot different when I left the stadium that day than other seasons, because we always seemed to lose in Minnesota."

Favre suffered a concussion against the New York Giants in 2004, then famously returned to throw a touchdown pass before the team forced him to sit. Favre also had right elbow tendinitis in both 2000 and 2010, yet played through both injuries.

"It's beyond reason. It's ridiculous," said Matt Hasselbeck, who backed Favre up in Green Bay. "He's just the toughest guy in the world."

I saw firsthand the recuperative powers of Favre from my broadcast location in Chicago. In a 1994 game at Minnesota, Favre missed most of the second half due to what was termed a severely bruised left hip.

The next week, the Packers played a Monday-night game in Soldier Field. The Bears were retiring the numbers of Hall of Famers Dick Butkus—my former broadcast partner—and Gale Sayers. It was a cold, windy, and rainy night on the lakefront, as miserable a night as there could be.

Lee Remmel, Green Bay's legendary public relations director and a gifted writer with a huge vocabulary, described the weather perfectly as "a cold, cyclonic rainstorm."

Playing on that bad hip, Favre rushed for a 36-yard touchdown, diving over a Bears defender into the end zone. Later, he hit running back Edgar Bennett on a 13-yard touchdown pass, staking the Packers to a 27–0 lead.

Green Bay would go on to win the game 33–6. Even at "less than" 100 percent, Favre was worth the price of admission. He always was.

The other lasting impression I had that evening was the halftime ceremony to retire Butkus' No. 51 and Sayers' No. 40. Then–team president Michael McCaskey was standing on the field with Butkus and Sayers with rain pelting them like machine-gun fire.

There was also no one in the stands, as everyone had gone underneath the seating area to take refuge from the elements. It was a sad sight to see, whether you were a Bears fan or not.

I also witnessed Favre's remarkable five-touchdown outing against Chicago on a bad ankle in 1995. Favre's status for the game was highly questionable, and most of us figured he would either not play or be severely limited, considering he had not practiced all week.

The words of NBA star Allen Iverson some years later put practice in a certain perspective: "We're talking about practice, man. We ain't talking about the game. We're talking about practice!"

Favre's performance against the Bears that day was the stuff of legend. He completed 25-of-33 passes for 336 yards with five touchdowns and no interceptions. Favre's quarterback rating that day of 147.2 was the highest of his career.

Green Bay notched a 35–28 victory on its way to its first NFC Central title since 1972. Practice? Favre proved he didn't need no stinkin' practice!

What motivates stars to play games even when they shouldn't? The superstars I have been around each had a different drive about them.

Former Bears running back Walter Payton felt a passionate duty to his team and a love of the game. Payton knew when he took the field that his teammates all believed they were going to win.

Payton also took his fierce motivation from the fact that coming out of high school, the larger colleges overlooked him. Payton went to a small school, Jackson State, and was not the top pick in the 1975 draft (he was taken No. 4 overall by the Bears).

These facts drove him to become one of the best football players of all time, if not the best. Payton missed just one game in his 13-year career, an astounding statistic for a running back.

Basketball's Michael Jordan played every night, even the exhibition games, for three reasons. First, he loved the game. Second, he had an unyielding need to compete—at basketball, cards, or just about anything presented him. And third, Jordan felt it was his obligation to the fans who came to see him play.

Jordan never forgot when he was demoted from varsity to JV as a freshman in high school. Jordan motivated himself through slights, some real, some imagined. Jordan was always construing the words of others—even words of praise—as a veiled slight and turning them into motivation.

But most of all Jordan just loved the game. He loved to compete. And as his dad once said, "Michael doesn't have a gambling problem. He has a competitive problem."

From what I could tell, Favre thoroughly enjoyed the game and competition, but fear was a part of the reason Brett played every game, because he actually worried about someone else taking his job.

Maybe it stemmed back to the 1994 season, when Favre and the Packers struggled for much of the year. Green Bay was 6–7 at one point, and coach Mike Holmgren had threatened to play backup Mark Brunell over Favre.

"Absolutely, I took that very seriously," Favre said. "It crossed my mind at times. And I placed a lot upon myself to right the ship, if you will. But there are also times when you can put too much pressure on yourself and that's a really bad thing. But there were times when I wondered if every play could be my last."

Green Bay rallied down the stretch, won its final three games to finish 9–7, and earned the top wild-card spot. The highlight came in a 21–17 win over Atlanta in the final game ever played at Milwaukee's County Stadium.

Trailing 17–14, the Packers drove to the Falcons' 9-yard line with 19 seconds left. Green Bay was out of timeouts as Favre came to the line for a third-and-2 play.

When no one came free, Favre took off on a mad scramble for the right corner of the end zone. Favre stumbled at the 6, regained his footing at the 3, and lunged for the goal line.

Had Favre been tackled short of the goal line, the game likely would have ended. Instead, Favre narrowly beat rookie cornerback Anthony Phillips to the end zone for a dramatic victory.

The Packers then defeated Detroit 16–12 in a wild-card game, and

Favre's job was secure for the rest of his tenure in Green Bay. But Favre never took anything for granted.

In some ways, Favre was the most insecure "superstar" I have ever been around. There were times in blowout situations when head coach Mike Sherman would want to take Favre out. Talk shows would admonish Sherman afterward for not pulling Favre with the Packers securely in front. What people didn't realize is Favre wouldn't come out!

Some of that insecurity might have come from Favre's father, Irv, who coached him extremely hard in high school. Or perhaps it stemmed from Holmgren's demanding ways early in Favre's career.

But Favre effectively channeled that insecurity into a competitive motivation that was second to none. Every day, every play, every snap, Favre had to be on the field leading his team. If he wasn't, he wondered if he would become the next Wally Pipp, a terrific first baseman for the New York Yankees in the early 1900s who lost his job to Lou Gehrig after an injury and never got it back.

Favre also remembered that he became the starter following an injury to Majkowski in 1992. Later in his career, Favre's insecurity led to some awkward moments between he and Aaron Rodgers, who was selected in the first round of the 2005 draft.

Each of these great athletes channeled their emotions into a driving force that catapulted them to the top of their profession.

Favre's flair for the dramatic is unprecedented in the Packers' long history. He led Green Bay on 40 game-winning drives, and had 45 total during his 20-year NFL career.

The thing about a "gunslinger" is he will shoot you either into a win or into a loss. There is no in-between.

Favre finished his Green Bay career with 160 wins, the most by a starting quarterback in NFL history at the time. He held the league mark for most touchdown passes in a career (442), but he also held the league mark for most interceptions with 288 (now 336, the most in NFL history).

How good was Favre? I thought the only one in the universe who would be "allowed" to throw six interceptions in a playoff game was God. I was wrong. Mike Sherman let Favre do exactly that in a divisional playoff loss at St. Louis in 2001.

The Rams returned three of the interceptions for touchdowns. And the Packers had eight turnovers that led to 35 St. Louis points.

"I could have thrown eight had we gotten the ball back," Favre said. "I was going to keep chucking."

Some of Favre's picks came at the most inopportune times. In the 2003 divisional playoffs in Philadelphia, Favre threw an inexplicable overtime interception to Brian Dawkins that set up a game-winning field goal for the Eagles.

Four years later in the NFC Championship Game against the New York Giants at Lambeau Field, Favre again made a brutal late-game mistake.

On Green Bay's first possession of overtime, Giants cornerback Corey Webster intercepted Favre. Moments later, New York kicker Lawrence Tynes drilled a 47-yard field goal and the Giants had a stunning win.

Amazingly, that pass intended for Driver—the one intercepted by Webster—was Favre's last in a Packers uniform. And two weeks later, the Giants won Super Bowl XLII.

"In some ways, it was a surprise to a lot of people we were in this game," Favre said. "Unfortunately, the last thing you remember usually is a game like tonight. For me, the last play. But there have been so many great achievements that will stand out."

The most enduring image I have of Favre came in Super Bowl XXXI, when he threw a 54-yard touchdown pass to Andre Rison to open the scoring. Favre, in his pure joy of the moment, pulled his helmet off his head, raised it high in the air with his right hand, and sprinted to the sideline.

Today that would be a penalty, as you can't take your helmet off in the field of play. To me, as a lifelong Packers follower, that one moment is where I realized that for the first time since Super Bowl II, the Pack was back.

I wasn't the only one who ranks that moment at the top of Favre's highlight reel.

"People have asked me what's my favorite moment of Brett Favre's career," Harlan said. "I really think it was the first touchdown in Super Bowl XXXI when he threw to Rison and he ran off the field with his helmet off. He looked like a kid running home to Mom with his first great report card.

"I was so nervous that morning, so nervous about us being in the Super Bowl, and it gave me confidence to see him throw the ball like that and then run off the field like that. That gave me a great feeling."

This was common behavior for Favre. It didn't matter how old he was. At times, Favre was like a giant child playing a man's game.

"The one thing I always heard people say and they still say it today is, 'I never saw someone play football and have more fun than Brett,'" Favre said. "And that's true. It was fun. It was a lot of fun. And I know my teammates would feed on that and the fans fed on it, too. It was fun. That's how it was. I would have done anything for my team."

Not all great quarterbacks make those around them better. Terry Bradshaw already had Hall of Fame receivers like Lynn Swann and John Stallworth on his side. Joe Montana had the greatest receiver in the history of the game, Jerry Rice, and two-time All-Pro John Taylor opposite him.

Those quarterbacks didn't have to make those guys better. They were already great.

Favre never had receivers of that caliber, with the exception of one.

The most talented receiver Favre played with in Green Bay was Sterling Sharpe. Favre played just three seasons with Sharpe, though, after the Pro Bowler was forced into early retirement due to a neck injury he suffered during the 1994 season. In just fewer than three seasons together, Favre and Sharpe hooked up on 41 touchdown passes.

Antonio Freeman caught 51 touchdown passes from Favre, but that came over an eight-year span. With all due respect, Favre took his receivers to a level they would have never reached without him.

"I was fortunate I got to play with Brett Favre for nine years," Rivera said. "His presence in the huddle, his leadership, it forced everybody to play better. You had to bring your 'A' game when you're going to be in Brett Favre's huddle."

Along the way, Favre helped Freeman become a two-time All-Pro, made Robert Brooks a star, turned tight end Mark Chmura into a Pro Bowler, helped Donald Driver become the all-time leading receiver in Packers history, and threw 19 touchdown passes to Bill Schroeder. The list goes on and on, too.

Each one of these players would tell you Favre made them better than they could ever be without him! Favre had the uncanny ability to raise not only his level of play, but the level of play of those around him. That is a rare trait, even for the most gifted of players.

"Brett Favre is one of the greatest quarterbacks in the history of professional football," said former Denver head coach Mike Shanahan, who led the Broncos past Favre's Packers in Super Bowl XXXII. "You're judged by winning, and he's won more games than any other quarterback who has ever played. He was the face of the Packers and a great credit to our game."

Favre's leadership was also vital to everything he did.

Irvin Favre—Brett's father—was the head football coach at Hancock North Central High School in Kiln, Mississippi. Brett quarterbacked the Hawks for three seasons when he reached high school. But well before that, Favre followed his father to football practice many days, and unbeknownst to him at the time, began learning leadership lessons that would help him later in life.

"Being around football from a young age, I was around black guys; I was around white guys; I was around football talk and some of the things that are said in the locker room," Favre said. "And there were things said in there that you would never say at home. That was kind of a sacred ground in the locker room.

"So I just kind of learned the ropes at an early age, being around my dad. And you don't know it at the time, but you're learning how to fit in with everyone. And I think I learned a lot of the qualities a good teammate should have."

In a melting-pot sport, Favre understood how vital it was to have a relationship with each and every one of his teammates. He was the glue—and he took that role seriously.

Those around him certainly noticed.

"Here's why there will never be another Brett Favre," former Packers safety LeRoy Butler said. "When Brett Favre got there, you had black guys playing a game of spades, white guys playing backgammon, the younger guys playing video games, the older guys playing hearts. And Brett fit in with every culture.

"He'd go over to the brothers and listen to hip-hop. He'd go over to the white guys and listen to country. He'd go hang out with the hunters, he'd go hang with the young guys. There was no guy that ever did that. Hell, I never did that.

"It's nice when organically, someone can fit in with everybody else and Brett did that. When he came in the locker room, he didn't wait for people to come over to him. He went over to people. And that wasn't publicized. He didn't want the publicity of that.

"But he was an unbelievable teammate. I'm telling you, no quarterback has ever done that, to realize there [are] so many different cultures in the locker room and he could fit in with all of them. And he fit in.

"He didn't even know how to play spades, but he'd be yelling, 'I got next.' He didn't even like hip-hop, but he would dance to it. He didn't want to get up at 4 in the morning to go hunting before practice at 9:00, but he did it. He didn't want to go to some of these functions with us, but he did it because he loved his teammates.

"I don't think there was ever a guy that loved his teammates more than Brett. It's impossible to think that someone could love his teammates more. I don't think anybody ever put more energy into loving his teammates than Brett did.

"You felt like if you were in a foxhole with somebody, I want a son-of-a-bitch that when I'm asleep won't put his gun down and will give his life for me. That's Brett Favre. That's Brett Favre. I want him in my foxhole.

"He used to give rookies his truck. Brand-new truck to run around in and he'd say, 'I can get another ride.' I mean, who does that? He got along with all the races, all the cultures. I mean, they broke the mold on Brett Favre."

During the 2007 season—Favre's final year in Green Bay—we were on "records watch" all season. Favre was coming up on two key all-time NFL marks—passing yardage and touchdown passes.

On September 30 at Minnesota, Favre passed Dan Marino on the all-time touchdown list when he hit Greg Jennings on a 16-yard scoring strike in the first quarter. It was the 421st touchdown pass of Favre's career.

"I've said this all along and will continue to say it, I've never considered myself in the same league as Dan Marino," Favre said that season.

"What a great passer, maybe the greatest passer ever.

"The way he did it is probably the way you would coach another guy to do it. The way I've done it, I don't know if you would coach guys to do it that way. But it's worked for me, and to be mentioned in the same breath with him is quite an honor."

Later that day, I said to Brett, "I'm glad it came early in the game and not with the game on the line." He said, "Me too." The point being, as an announcer, you want that record-setting play to stand alone so you can give it its due.

They stopped the game for an announcement, and of course, the ball used for that touchdown was taken out of the game. I know some feel it would be much more dramatic if it was part of a last-second throw to win the game. But in that case, the record took a backseat to the outcome of the game.

Favre also passed Marino later that season and became the NFL's all-time leader in career passing yards, passing attempts, and completions.

Of all the great Favre plays, moments, and games, though, nothing compares to what I witnessed on December 22, 2003.

We were in Oakland for a Monday night-game against the Raiders. That weekend, Brett's dad, Irv, a friend to us all, passed away from a heart attack.

One day after Irv's death, Favre decided to play in a game the Packers desperately needed to win to keep their playoff hopes alive. In a somewhat unprecedented moment in the long history of the Oakland Coliseum, aka the "Black Hole," Raiders fans cheered Favre when he took the field for pregame introductions.

Favre then threw four touchdowns and for 399 yards and led the Packers to an unforgettable 41–7 win over Oakland on *Monday Night Football*. Favre honored his father with one of the most remarkable performances of his career.

And NFL Network recently voted this the No. 1 game of Favre's magnificent career.

"The previous day when I got the news is all kind of a blur," Favre said. "But the game itself, much like the way I played, is still really clear. The flow of emotions was much like a roller coaster. You throw a touchdown and it's a total high. Then you go back to the sidelines and it hits you again, and you start thinking that you have to fly home after the game and your dad is going to be buried. That's tough and this is all going on during the game.

"But when I was playing, when I was in the game, I was really zeroed in on what I had to do, as hard as that might be. So it was up and down, up and down, back and forth."

Favre played in 277 games during his 16 years in Green Bay, including the playoffs. But his passer rating of 154.9 that night was the best of his Packers career.

"I've never seen a leader or a player like Brett in my career, and I'm pretty sure that nobody else in this locker room has," former Packers tight end Wesley Walls said. "I think we wanted to make him proud. Just getting up in front of the team at such a horrible and difficult time in his life really showed he cared about us. That was something I'll never forget."

Packers wide receiver Antonio Freeman couldn't believe what he saw, either.

"What he had to deal with was [immeasurable]," Freeman said. "You can't put a price on what he did. I don't know how he did it, but he did it in fine fashion."

Favre's receivers did their part, too, reaching up into the damp Bay Area air to make one great catch after another.

Javon Walker had touchdown grabs of 43 and 23 yards, as well as a 46-yard reception. Robert Ferguson caught passes of 47 and 27 yards. Walls snared a memorable 22-yard touchdown pass in the back of the end zone on a play that appeared to have little chance of success. And Donald Driver had receptions of 41 and 32 yards.

Favre completed his first nine passes and threw for a personal-best 311 yards and four touchdowns in the first half alone. He also finished the first half with a perfect passer rating of 158.3.

"We had a meeting with the receiving corps and made a pact that whatever he put up, we were going to come down with," Ferguson said. "We rallied around our leader."

I don't know how a person plays through the kind of grief Favre had to be experiencing that night, but it was another testament to his incredible inner toughness. And I'll bet Irv was all smiles watching from his new perch in paradise.

"I just know this: my dad wouldn't have wanted me to play. He would have *demanded* that I play," Favre said. "So I didn't know what to do for a while. I wanted to play and I wanted to honor my dad, but I wasn't sure how I'd play. But my prayers were answered."

When I was growing up in Massachusetts, the excellence of the Lombardi Packers poured through our new color television set, and the Packers became a "national" team. By the time Favre arrived in Green Bay, it had been almost a quarter of a century since the Packers had been relevant nationally in terms of championships.

Favre changed all of that, not only by his play on the field and making Green Bay relevant again, but also by his exuberance and style.

Yes, the gunslinger was great entertainment. And to be honest, that is what sports is all about today.

Major sports cannot rely on simply the die-hard fans. They aren't a big enough audience.

For most watching on television, even a good portion of those at the games, sports is a form of entertainment. That's all it is!

So it is no longer good enough to just win. You must be compelling to watch.

Sports today, especially on television, relies on a wide cross section of society that just wants to have fun, either at the game or watching at home. Brett Favre was fun to watch, and boy, did he entertain.

The Packers, and Favre, captured that national audience again in the 1990s like Lombardi's Packers had in the 1960s, largely because Favre was compelling to watch.

"As you get older, as we all get older, you learn to appreciate things more," Favre said. "And I think experience plays a big part of that, and obviously at 22, 23, 24, I didn't have that. But I was always a historian and really a respectful player. And I knew what the guys had done before and I understood how lucky I was to do it. So I kind of knew I was part of something special even as it was going on.

"It had been so long since the Packers had any success, and to be part of teams that got things turned around and going in the right direction was really special. That whole period was something special. And I know I appreciate it now more than I did back then. I don't want to say it was easy, but for a lack of a better term, that's what I felt. What's the big deal? We're just winning games and doing what we're supposed to.

"I hope I did my part. I believe I did. I think I was part of something that was very special and returned the franchise back to prominence. And I take tremendous amount of pride in that. By no means do I think I did that alone. I was a part of one of the greatest teams and greatest groups of guys that's played in Green Bay."

I loved calling Favre's games with the Packers. As a lifelong follower of the team, I appreciate the talent he brought to Green Bay, his flair for the dramatic, and the pure joy with which he played the game.

I am sure some have played this great game with as much joy as Favre did. But I never saw anyone play the game with more.

"I think the thing that means the most is when people tell me, 'I love watching how you play because that's how I'd play,'" Favre said. "They always talk about how much fun I was having. That's pretty neat. That's fun. I think people could relate to me and that really means the most. That's what I love to hear."

CHAPTER 5
MIKE SHERMAN

In this business, you have professional relationships of varying degrees with people ranging from general managers and scouts to coaches and players.

Most of the time, professional courtesy is all that is needed or accomplished between a reporter and the individuals he or she covers. For the most part, NFL head coaches are hard to get close to. They are responsible for a 53-man roster, at least 20 assistant coaches and staff members, and of course, the performance of their team.

Coaches operate in a pressure cooker and must coach to the lowest common denominator on their squad. Some handle this better than others. Most of them are control freaks that take an "us against the world" approach with anyone who is not in uniform. In some ways, the job demands they take this type of stance both on and off the field.

In effect, that means some coaches believe they need to be jerks. This carries into their relationships with the media as well. Sometimes it is not very pleasant to be around these people.

Anyone who has watched New England coach Bill Belichick conduct a midweek press conference can see the disdain he has for these events and the people asking the questions.

Belichick frowns. His mutterings are barely audible. He looks almost slovenly in his cut-off hoodie. It doesn't paint a glowing picture of either Belichick or his organization.

The only reason an owner like Robert Kraft allows someone like Belichick to represent his organization this way is because the coach has won four Super Bowls. Winning in sports trumps everything and everyone!

The NFL is a copycat league, and when Belichick started winning Super Bowls, every Tom, Dick, and Harry in the league started to emulate the New England coach and the charades he plays with the media. Some even wore the hooded sweatshirt as they mumbled nonanswers to questions asked by the reporters.

Former Green Bay coach Mike Sherman became quite adept at letting the media know just how much he resented the time he had to give them. For Sherman and most head coaches, any time they had to spend away from the Xs and Os of football was superfluous.

Forget the fact the media is simply a conduit between the team and the fans. The Green Bay Packers are also owned by the fans. Sherman never seemed to grasp that concept, and his responsibility of communicating with his "owners."

Sherman once went ballistic when someone's cell phone went off during one of his press conferences, then demanded the guilty party step up and accept his wrath and blame publicly. Sherman loved to embarrass members of the press whenever he could, and I speak from experience!

It was comical that during those years Sherman railed against the intrusion of cell phones, yet he did a television commercial for Cellcom in Green Bay. A contrast, to say the least.

After many of his press briefings, Sherman would retreat back to the locker room. He was once overheard remarking to public relations director Jeff Blumb, "Well, I guess I gave them nothing today." The two would have a nice chuckle about the exchange and go on their way.

During the days of Bob Harlan and Ron Wolf, there was always a certain amount of transparency in the Packers' public responses to the media. They seemed to understand that any time a coach or team official is speaking on the record to anyone in the media, he or she is speaking to the fan base.

How those officials relate to the media can have a positive or negative impact on how the individual or the team is perceived by the paying customers. There is a way of not giving away "state secrets" and yet answering a question in a pleasant manner that makes the reporter and his readers or audience feel like they are worth the time.

In theory, I should have had an extremely close professional relationship with Sherman. We are the same age, both grew up in Massachusetts, both became Packers fans in the 1960s, and had both followed the team ever since. We had a lot of similarities, with the exception that he is a Red Sox fan and I am a Yankees fan. When it comes to the greatest rivalry in all of baseball, I guess that means something.

In March, after Sherman was named head coach of the Packers, my wife, Julie, and I sat at the Lombardi Awards Dinner in Milwaukee with Sherman and his wife, Karen. We had a great time and a wonderful conversation. From there, everything in my relationship with Sherman went downhill.

I suspect most of the fallout was on me. I went into our interview situations expecting to work with the Mike Sherman I met at that dinner, and what I eventually got was a totally different person.

It certainly didn't help that I was a few minutes late to an interview, and once my cell phone went off during a media session with the coach. So I will accept that my lack of professionalism in those instances probably led to our rocky relationship.

Before each Packers game, I do an interview with the head coach. It runs about six minutes and airs about 40 minutes before kickoff.

Game-day morning is not an especially pleasant time to visit with an NFL head coach. The pressure of the upcoming game weighs heavily on these people. Many coaches understand that this interview, usually done with a member of the broadcast team, is not a journalistic effort. Some, like Coach Sherman, never understood the place this pregame interview had in the process.

Sherman used to have me come to his office in Green Bay four hours ahead of kickoff. So if the game was at noon, I had to be at Lambeau Field at 8:00 am. If I knocked on his door two or three minutes late, he was perturbed. If I knocked on his door two or three minutes early, he was equally agitated.

So I would sit in his outer office and watch the clock until it struck 8:00 exactly. Sherman was easily the least pleasant person I have ever interviewed on game day.

There was rarely an interview we did that wouldn't need editing, because he didn't like my question or wasn't satisfied with his own response to a question. It complicated our engineer Scott Pfeifer's morning. By contrast, Mike McCarthy's pregame interview has been edited twice in 10 years. Oh, by the way—McCarthy and I tape our pregame interview 90 minutes before kickoff in an office across the hall from the Packers locker room at Lambeau Field.

I guess when I asked Sherman something, he felt like I was challenging him. I was simply trying to get some insight for our listeners. But he didn't seem to understand that at all. I've never been around another head coach who had that same level of apprehension in a simple interview situation.

Before and after the interview—again, done four hours before kickoff—I noticed Sherman and offensive coordinator Tom Rossley appeared to still be working on the play sheet for that game! They had spent all week, 16 hours a day, working on the game plan, and from what it looked like they still weren't done on Sunday morning.

You talk about a guy overpreparing—about paralysis by analysis. That was Mike Sherman. It's remarkable to me that Sherman and Rossley would still be putting together the game plan—on game day!

Sherman was known as a "grinder" in the business. He was one of the best coaches I have ever been around in terms of preparing a team during the week of the game.

But I do believe he either had insecurity issues or he was such a perfectionist that whatever they came up with, no matter how long it took, was not good enough. Maybe he was insecure in how he got the job as the Packers' head coach in the first place.

In his first stint in Green Bay in the late 1990s, Sherman was the tight ends coach and spent most of his time either on the field or locked in a closet studying film. Sherman never had to deal with the other demands a head coach faces—non-football-related duties and interacting with people, especially outside the organization.

Sherman went to Seattle with Mike Holmgren in 1999 as the offensive coordinator, but Holmgren called the plays.

Green Bay fired head coach Ray Rhodes following a disappointing 8–8 season in 1999. During interviews for the Packers' head coaching vacancy, Sherman impressed general manager Ron Wolf by showing up for his interview with an entire plan for the upcoming year—every day, every practice, every drill! Wolf was reportedly blown away and hired Sherman for the job as head coach of the Green Bay Packers.

Let's understand one thing about Mike Sherman: he was a very good coach and won a lot of games in Green Bay. Sherman was the best preparer of a football team I think I've ever seen. He left no stone unturned. He was meticulous in getting his team ready week in and week out.

Sherman's mentality was, *I'm going to outwork you. You might be more talented than me or smarter than me, but I'm going to outwork you.* He gets a lot of credit for that.

But game-day decisions—things like fourth-and-26 or fourth-and-1 earlier in that same fourth quarter of that 2003 playoff game in Philadelphia—is where Mike Sherman was not nearly as good. Even if he was "just" the coach, and the general manager put better players around him, the game-day element was always going to hold Mike Sherman back. Coach Sherman was never going to take the Packers to the Promised Land.

Despite all of that, Sherman had a good amount of success on the field.

After an 0–2 start to the 2000 campaign, Sherman's Packers responded, and the club won nine of its last 14 games, finishing the year on a four-game winning streak. There was a positive vibe in Green Bay about Sherman and the Packers thanks to that finish.

Then, Wolf retired as GM following the 2001 season. Packers president and CEO Bob Harlan knew the best way to structure his team was to have a general manager who would oversee the head coach.

Harlan, like many, though, was very high on Sherman and decided it

Mike Sherman the general manager played a large role in getting Mike Sherman the coach fired.

would be wrong to name a GM "over" him. So Harlan went against his management instinct—he made Sherman both coach and GM.

Just when Sherman was growing into a first-rate head coach and feeling good about his new job, he was given another one. Now, with the pressure of the dual role, Sherman became borderline insufferable, at least from my perspective.

Sherman's Packers continued to win, going 12–4 in both 2001 and 2002. But a postseason loss to Michael Vick and the Atlanta Falcons following the 2002 season, the first playoff loss Green Bay ever experienced on Wisconsin soil, began Sherman's unraveling.

Sherman had final say in the draft room, and did not have much regard for the opinions of the people who studied the players and prepared for the college draft year round. The opinions of people such as John Schneider, Reggie McKenzie, and John Dorsey, all of whom helped build the Super Bowl XLV–champion Packers, were undervalued. Professionally, they were all frustrated by Sherman the GM. Today, each of those men is a general manager in the NFL.

Dorsey told me that on draft day, Sherman simply didn't listen to the people whose business it was to know college talent. And that was a major mistake. Dorsey and McKenzie and Schneider and Shaun Herock knew what they were doing. They knew talent.

In fairness to Sherman the GM, in May 2001, shortly after he took on the job, the Packers hired an experienced personnel and front office operative, Mark Hatley, as their vice president of football operations. I got to know "Hat" while he was vice president of player personnel of the Chicago Bears. He was extremely talented, loved throughout the Packers organization, and was one of the few people in the front office who had Sherman's ear. Hatley died unexpectedly of heart failure in July 2004. Without question, the void in the front office left by his passing played a role in the eventual demise of Sherman the general manager.

As soon as the football season concluded, Sherman threw himself into reviewing tape and forming his own opinions on player personnel, both college and pro. His evaluations were often at odds with what his people were telling him. Sherman continued trying to build the Packers around Brett Favre, before the great quarterback's window of Super Bowl opportunity closed.

During the draft, rather than taking the best player available regardless of position, Sherman traded draft choices to move up for a player he needed that minute. To use a baseball metaphor, he was always trying to hit a home run when all he needed was a base hit.

Sherman's machinations left him with just six players in the 2002 draft. His 2003 draft was a complete washout. And when Sherman began the 2004 draft with cornerbacks Ahmad Carroll and Joey Thomas, defensive lineman Donnell Washington, and punter B.J. Sander, his days as a general manager were numbered.

Sherman bombed with free-agent signings, such as defensive end Joe Johnson in 2002. That season, Johnson tore his left triceps in the second half of a win at Chicago on October 7 and was lost for the year. The following season, Johnson made just six tackles with no sacks, and his time in Green Bay was over.

Johnson never wanted to leave New Orleans, and never fit in with Green Bay. Free agency is a perilous business in so many ways. Sherman went to New Orleans personally to recruit Johnson. But sometimes, no matter how talented a free agent might be, he also might not fit the scheme, the culture of the team, or the community. Unfortunately for Johnson and the Packers, he missed on all three.

Sherman the general manager was building a roster around Favre, at the expense of building a team that would be a contender year after year.

By the end of a difficult 2004 season, Harlan realized Sherman could no longer handle both jobs. The Packers were 10–6 that season and reached the postseason for a fourth straight year. But the team was aging rapidly, and Sherman's inadequate drafts left the roster devoid of young talent.

51

Harlan was also bothered by an exchange he had with Sherman in early October 2004. Harlan and Sherman met on a Saturday just 24 hours before Green Bay had a big game with the New York Giants.

Instead of concentrating on the Giants, Sherman was spending his day focusing on cornerback Mike McKenzie, who was in the middle of a lengthy holdout. (Sherman eventually traded McKenzie to New Orleans.)

But when Harlan left that meeting, he realized Sherman simply had too much on his plate.

"I thought, 'You know, with a big game coming up tomorrow, we need to be focused in. Somebody else can do these things,'" Harlan said. "And so it was just these situations where I thought, 'If I had another person in the football mode, he could do those things and let Mike coach.' I think this helps prolong his career."

It didn't.

After the 2004 season, Harlan hired Ted Thompson as Green Bay's general manager. Thompson inherited a roster that lacked young talent.

Thompson immediately became Sherman's boss, as well. And that relationship was a bust from the start.

Sherman just couldn't get over losing the general manager job. And rather than taking it as a chance to focus on coaching, he took Thompson's presence as a personal affront.

Mike Sherman was a very proud person, and he was stubborn. He never gave Ted Thompson the time of day.

Thompson just never felt welcomed to visit with Sherman.

Sherman's relationship with Bob Harlan changed, as well. A once-close connection between the two became strained.

By that point, Sherman had also driven away several of his assistant coaches. Many of them took lateral positions with different organizations simply because working with Sherman became untenable.

"The head coach thought he was the only one with any brains," said

Johnny Roland, who spent the 2004 season coaching Green Bay's running backs. "There was a lot of collective knowledge in the people that have left. And that knowledge wasn't listened to."

Roland said aside from offensive coordinator Tom Rossley and former special teams consultant Frank Novak, Sherman rarely listened to anyone on the staff.

"There were a lot of guys that have been around a long time," said Roland, who was an NFL assistant from 1976 to 2005. "You think they should have a little bit of input into how this game should be played and things you should take advantage of. But that wasn't how it worked up there."

The result? High turnover among assistant coaches.

"Why do you think those guys left?" queried former Packers tight ends coach Jeff Jagodzinski. "It wasn't to go to a better team. It's because in Green Bay, your ideas don't get listened to.

"In Green Bay, a lot of guys bite their tongues on a lot of things. If you're in an organization, you want to feel that you're a part of it. And when you don't have any decision-making responsibilities or they don't take your suggestions or whatever, that's frustrating."

Eventually, Sherman was silenced as well.

Before the 2005 season, Thompson gave Sherman a two-year contract extension. But at the conclusion of Green Bay's 4–12 year, Thompson fired Sherman.

"Decisions like this are never easy," Thompson said on the day he fired Sherman. "They require a lot of thought and consternation, but at the end of the day, I thought we needed to go in a different direction."

The head coach makes a huge difference in the direction and the attitude and the confidence of the team. And Sherman had lost that team by the end.

Later that week, Sherman met with the media one final time and showed a sense of humor that had been in mothballs for six years.

"Hope you all put away your cell phones," he joked.

I still think if Sherman had been "just" the coach—and not the general manager, too—he would have been fine. He could have been more successful. The guys in the front office would have gotten Sherman better players than the ones he went after. That's the trick.

In hindsight, I believe what primarily doomed Sherman in Green Bay is a malady that can damn any executive in any business—micromanagement. Sherman had to have his hands in everything involving the football operation.

Additionally, as several of his former coaches have pointed out over the years, he had a "trust" issue. He did not trust the people around him—even those whom he had hired—so he didn't value their opinions. In many ways he became an island unto himself.

It appeared to me that Sherman believed only in his undying work ethic. If he could outwork everyone, that would lead to success. In pro sports—in any business today involving a team—no one individual can do it all.

To borrow a quote my broadcast partner, Larry McCarren, has used on other occasions, "We haven't cornered the market on brains, brawn, and hard work." In the NFL, no one has.

CHAPTER 6
BEFORE FOURTH-AND-26

Before fourth-and-26, the Packers had won three games in a row. On the final week of the 2003 regular season, Green Bay needed a win over a disinterested, playoffs-bound Denver Broncos and a Minnesota Vikings loss at Phoenix to the lowly Cardinals.

The Packers did their part, blasting the Broncos 31–3 as Denver coach Mike Shanahan rested his starters for the AFC playoff run. A four-game winning streak helped the Packers finish the regular season at 10–6 after a disappointing 4–5 start.

But Green Bay still needed help from an unlikely source. A Minnesota win at Arizona would send the Vikings to the postseason instead of the Packers. But the Cardinals were double-digit underdogs that day, leaving Packer Nation with little faith.

Amazingly, though, the Cardinals gave the Vikings all they could handle. And virtually none of the 70,000 fans inside Lambeau Field knew what was happening.

Smartphones weren't ubiquitous back in 2003. And Packers coach Mike Sherman had ordered that the Vikings score be kept off the Jumbotron so his players wouldn't be distracted.

"We knew (Sherman) took it off the board…but basically you just paid attention to the crowd," Packers running back Tony Fisher said. "And when you saw the crowd erupting, you knew something good was happening."

With Green Bay's game well in hand, though, everyone was searching for ways to follow the Vikings game. Many in club seats had the game on their televisions, and word filtered through the stadium.

In fact, Larry McCarren and I also began broadcasting the Vikings game to the statewide audience from a television we were watching in the press box. And what everyone experienced was a magical moment.

Trailing 17–12, Arizona had time for one final play from Minnesota's 28-yard line. Cardinals quarterback Josh McCown took the last snap with four seconds left on the clock, then avoided trouble by rolling to his right.

McCown found little-used wideout Nathan Poole in the right corner of the end zone. Poole made a spectacular grab, got one foot down, then was pushed out of bounds by Minnesota's Denard Walker and Brian Russell.

Poole's touchdown was under review for four minutes, and after much deliberation, it was ruled he was forced out of bounds while making the catch. The touchdown stood. The Cardinals had won!

Green Bay's game ended at virtually the same time, and the Packers knew by watching their fans and via reports from upstairs that they were NFC North champions.

Brett Favre raised his arms to the sky, then teared up. Sherman was doused with a bucket of water. And Lambeau Field became bedlam.

"I had no idea what was going on and it was mad confusion," right guard Marco Rivera said. "Then I saw the crowd react and I thought, 'What the hell's wrong with the crowd? The game's not going on. Is there a fight over there?'

"Then I finally asked [director of football administration] Bruce Warwick and he said, 'Oh my God! Arizona just scored.' It was unbelievable. We were in the playoffs."

Green Bay was in, and was also red hot.

Before fourth-and-26, the Packers battled the Seattle Seahawks into overtime in a legendary wild-card playoff game at Lambeau Field.

The teams ended regulation tied 27–27. Seattle then won the coin toss at the outset of overtime.

Seahawks quarterback Matt Hasselbeck, a former Packer, famously said, "We want the ball and we're gonna score!" That bombastic comment was picked up by the official's microphone and heard in living rooms across the country.

On Seattle's second possession of overtime, Hasselbeck threw a pass to the left side intended for wideout Alex Bannister. Packers cornerback Al Harris jumped the route and motored 52 yards down the east sidelines into the north end zone, with his dreadlocks flying in his wake.

It was the first defensive touchdown to win an overtime playoff game in NFL history. That play sent the Packers to Philadelphia for the divisional round.

"I jumped a lot of routes," Harris said afterward. "(Hasselbeck) made a lot of good reads because I jumped a lot of routes today and he would look it off and go to the guy that was open.

"I was just praying that he would throw the ball, because I knew I was going to gamble on that play. As a DB, you pray that they will run that route—a hitch or a slant—something you can jump quick and get to where you have to go."

Before fourth-and-26, the Packers took a 14–0 lead in the divisional playoff game the following week at Philadelphia. Green Bay was dominating the game, and an NFC Championship Game at Carolina was seemingly in its future.

Before fourth-and-26, Green Bay had a fourth-and-1 at the Philadelphia 1-yard line just before halftime. The Packers led 14–7 at the time, but running back Ahman Green was stuffed by linebacker Mark Simoneau, and defensive end Jerome McDougal and the Eagles dodged a near-fatal dagger.

Before fourth-and-26 there was head coach Mike Sherman declaring to his squad at halftime, "If we get fourth-and-one again, we're going for it and we're going to ride your backs [offensive line] all the way to the Super Bowl!"

Before fourth-and-26 the Packers got another shot at fourth-and-1, this time from the Eagles' 41-yard line.

Leading 17–14 with just over two minutes left in the game and Eagles coach Andy Reid running out of timeouts, the Packers were poised to continue a physical, ball-control, time-consuming drive. Behind the best offensive line the Packers had put together since the Lombardi era, they had the Eagles on skates.

That line featured Chad Clifton in his prime at left tackle, athletic and feisty Mike Wahle at left guard, versatile Mike Flanagan at center, tough guy Marco Rivera at right guard, and scrappy Mark Tauscher at right tackle. Ahman Green was at his all-time best, rushing for 1,883 yards in 2003, the most in a single season in team history.

Sherman called a timeout, and on the air in the radio booth, during the timeout, both Larry McCarren and I said, "We would go for it!" We don't often criticize or predict play calls in our broadcast but I felt it was important to go on record before this crucial play not knowing what Sherman and his coaching staff had made up their mind to do.

The Packers came out and tried to draw the tired, depleted Eagles front four offsides and pick up the first down via penalty. But the Eagles front four was so exhausted it couldn't even jump, much less jump offsides. And here was the best Green Bay running game, behind the best offensive line since the Lombardi Packers, needing just one yard, three feet, 36 inches to essentially put the game out of reach. And they never snapped the football!

When the Eagles didn't (couldn't) jump offsides Sherman called another timeout, then sent in punter Josh Bidwell and watched him boot one into the end zone.

Now, we truly saw Mike Sherman for who he was. He was not the bold, impassioned orator of the halftime locker room promising to "go for it and we will ride your backs to the Super Bowl." Moments like these reveal the fiber of a coach in the fourth quarter of a playoff game—well before fourth-and-26 ever happened.

Relieved that they had dodged another dagger, the Eagles offense came back on the field at their 21-yard line needing just a field goal to tie. The drive started with a 22-yard run by Duce Staley.

On the next play, quarterback Donovan McNabb threw incomplete. A false start backed Philadelphia up five yards, and on the ensuing play, a sack pushed the Eagles back to their own 25-yard line. McNabb threw incomplete on third down, setting up fourth-and-26.

Freddie Mitchell's 15 seconds of fame came when he hauled in a 28-yard reception on fourth-and-26.

Just 1:12 remained, and the Eagles were out of timeouts. A math professor at the University of Wisconsin–Green Bay later calculated the odds of the Eagles picking up a first down as 1-in-339. But to the shock and dismay of Packer Nation, this was the Eagles' lucky day.

The play was "74 Double Go," calling for a 25-yard slant route for wide receiver Freddie Mitchell. McNabb threw a perfect strike to

Mitchell deep into the Packers secondary. The Green Bay "Cover 2" package was breaking down.

Middle linebacker Nick Barnett, who had shallow coverage of Mitchell, bit on the tight end and left his zone. Inexplicably, safeties Darren Sharper and Marques Anderson dropped 30 yards deep into coverage.

The only player that was close to making a play was safety Bhawoh Jue. He was playing the sidelines as is customary in Cover 2, but Jue was too late to prevent the catch or first down.

Mitchell leaped into the air, caught the football, and came crashing down with a soon-to-be-historic first down at the Packers' 46-yard line.

Green Bay seemed disorganized before fourth down, though, which led to much second-guessing later.

"Quite frankly, we should have called a timeout," cornerback Michael Hawthorne said. "We should have called timeout to regroup and play the defense that we know will make them catch everything in front of us."

After fourth-and-26, completions to Mitchell and Todd Pinkston and a McNabb scramble for another first down against a dispirited Green Bay defense set up David Akers' 37-yard field goal that tied the game 17–17 at the end of regulation.

After fourth-and-26, the Packers stopped the Eagles on their first possession of overtime. But on Green Bay's first play from scrimmage in the extra session, Favre threw an inexplicable pop fly down the far sidelines that was intercepted by Eagles safety Brian Dawkins and returned to the Packers' 34-yard line. Five plays later, Akers drilled a 31-yard field goal and won it for Philadelphia 20–17.

"I still think we could have won the Super Bowl that year," Sharper later said. "Everything was set up for us.

"We were playing great and had a ton of confidence. Our next game (at Carolina) was against a team we all felt we matched up really well against. But as we all know, fourth-and-26 ..."

After fourth-and-26, Packers defensive coordinator Ed Donatell—an excellent coordinator and a good man—was fired.

To this day, Donatell insists he wouldn't have done anything differently. He just would have coached it differently.

"I'd coach Nick Barnett to stay back deeper, I'd tell Bhawoh Jue to have awareness, and I'd tell Darren Sharper to buy that route at 20 yards," Donatell said. "But I'm not blaming any player. I'm not blaming any assistant. The buck stops with me. Somewhere along the line, the buck's got to stop and it's stopping right on me. I'm blaming myself for the way that was coached."

I have always maintained that the decisive play of that game was not fourth-and-26. It was fourth-and-1 at the Eagles' 41-yard line. Pick up that first down against a gagging Eagles defense and fourth-and-26 never happens.

I'm not sure that if he had to do it over again, Mike Sherman would change anything about that fourth-and-1 in the divisional playoff game at Philadelphia.

But I believe that play, not fourth-and-26, is what cost a very good Packers team an opportunity to advance to the NFC Championship Game. And it spoke volumes about the coach who made the decision to punt in that situation.

I think Mike Sherman lost the confidence of observers and his team that day in Philadelphia. From that day forward, I was convinced Mike Sherman could not lead the Packers back to the Promised Land.

DAGGER

People ask me all the time where the term *dagger* came from.

It is actually an old basketball term we used in the NBA. When someone would hit a shot—usually a three pointer—that put a team ahead by at least two possessions and not enough time for the other team to catch up, I would exclaim, "And there is your dagger!"

I was by no means the first to use this phrase. But I might have been the first to use it on a regular basis in football. At least, that's what I'm told.

The first time I ever uttered the phrase in a football game was October 14, 2001. The Packers were playing the defending World Champion Baltimore Ravens at Lambeau Field.

In the fourth quarter, Green Bay had a 24–10 lead when Brett Favre hit Bubba Franks on a 21-yard touchdown pass, putting the Packers ahead 31–10 with just 6:59 to go. I just had a feeling that score would hold up and I declared, "And there is your dagger!" The reference took off from there.

Now when the Packers win, everyone wants to know which play was the dagger. I always chuckle to myself. Those people obviously weren't listening to our broadcast, or didn't listen very well.

Score is not the only factor that goes into my call of the dagger. I have a gut feeling about how a game is going based on what I have observed. There are times when the dagger is seen by some as being premature. Many are uncomfortable, believing if I call the dagger too early, it will "jinx" the Packers.

But in all of the years I have used the term, the only time it didn't hold up was in Seattle during the controversial "Fail Mary" Monday-night game on September 24, 2012.

The dagger had already been thrown with the Packers leading 12–7 in the final minute of the game. On the last play of regulation,

Seattle quarterback Russell Wilson threw a Hail Mary into the end zone intended for wide receiver Golden Tate.

Both Tate and Packers defender M.D. Jennings got their hands on the ball, and both players were still in the air and attempting to gain position. The two replacement officials near the play initially gave separate signals of touchdown and touchback, before ruling the players had simultaneous possession, resulting in a Seattle touchdown.

The replay showed Jennings with the ball first, but the league failed to overturn through replay. I believe they feared a riot at CenturyLink Field if they overturned that call.

Prior to the catch, Tate had shoved Sam Shields out of the way in what the league later stated should have been offensive pass interference, which would have nullified the touchdown and resulted in a Green Bay victory. However, replay cannot be used to determine pass interference.

In the end, the Seahawks won 14–12. So I guess, technically, the dagger came out. But in reality, it should have been a Green Bay win, so I don't count it.

Oh, by the way, that game ended the NFL's use of replacement officials that season. The following week, the league came to terms with its striking regular officials and an ugly chapter in league annals came to an end.

The earliest I have ever delivered the dagger was on November 7, 2010, against the Dallas Cowboys. Right before halftime, Nick Collins scooped up a fumble by Dallas return man Bryan McCann, bringing it back to the south end zone for a 28–0 Green Bay lead with 2:04 to go in the second quarter.

It has gotten to the point where now if for some reason I don't use the term in a Packers win, people get upset with me. Some games don't have a dagger, mostly because the game was out of hand way too early or the closeness of the game left no singular decisive moment.

Sometimes the moment is so big, the result of the play so obvious, I don't add a dagger. A case in point came in 2015, when Aaron Rodgers threw that miracle Hail Mary to Richard Rodgers to beat the Lions in Detroit.

I didn't use the dagger call that night. That was such a shocking and incredible play that I let it stand on its own. Being totally truthful, I was trying to make sure I had the right player catching the pass. From our vantage point at Ford Field, all I could see was about three Packers going up for the ball. I had to wait to see who actually had it.

We were down near the 25-yard line that night and screened by the white Green Bay jerseys going up for the ball. So I was a bit hesitant until we were sure it was Richard Rodgers who caught the pass.

Television replays, even the home and national radio booths, were all closer to the 50-yard line and had a clearer view of that play. Some criticized me for not going ballistic on the call of that play.

The worst thing a play-by-play announcer can do on a huge play like that is get the number wrong. In other words, you have to have the correct names first and foremost! Also, a lot of people were looking for the dagger at the end of that call.

What's funny about the heat I took for that call is that later in the season, ESPN used our Packers Radio Network play-by-play call of the Rodgers-to-Rodgers heroics on their playoff promotion commercial.

As for the "dagger" call, remember: it is not just about score or time in the game. It's about a feel by me, for how the game is going and how it will end.

CHAPTER 7
TED THOMPSON AND
THE PACKERS WAY

E very successful organization has its "way."
Loosely translated, the way is a mission statement that guides an organization or a football operation in its decision-making processes.

Fans often take this to the next level in a "we are holier than thou" approach. Or, to steal a phrase from the Ronald Regan era, we're the "white house up on the hill."

Trust me; in the NFL, no one lives in a white house up on a hill when it comes to trying to put together a winning team.

From a football standpoint, this current Packers Way began with Ron Wolf in the early 1990s, when then–team president Bob Harlan gave Wolf full control over the football operation. Ted Thompson was one of Wolf's scouts, and Thompson has said many times he learned a great deal about the NFL from the Hall of Famer. Not a bad guy to learn from!

Thompson was first hired in Green Bay in 1992 as Green Bay's assistant director of pro personnel. After just one year with Green Bay, Thompson was promoted to director of pro personnel. Then, in 1997, Thompson was again promoted to director of player personnel, which involved overseeing all college and pro scouting operations.

There were countless weekends when Thompson and Wolf were the only two people in the building, watching film, film, and more film. And that often gave Thompson plenty of time to pick Wolf's brain on anything and everything pertaining to football.

"He'd talk about the history of the game and Bronco Nagurski and things like that," Thompson said of Wolf. "Or the history of the Packers. During some of those conversations I would ask [questions] and I think that's the way a person learns is you ask questions of someone who has those kinds of opinions.

"And I'd say, 'Well, how do you do this?' or 'What about that time we were in the draft and nobody could agree and then you guys went in the room and talked about it? How do you do that?' So a lot of his ideas and philosophies obviously are mine now."

Thompson seemed in line to eventually replace Wolf. But in April 1999, Wolf did longtime friend Ken Herock a favor, and hired him as Green Bay's vice president of personnel.

That placed Herock above Thompson on the food chain, a move Thompson admits he was stung by. Their relationship is fine today, but when Seattle offered Thompson its vice president of football operations position in January 2000, he jumped at it.

"I left here because the opportunity to do what I did in Seattle was just too great to turn down," Thompson said. "Knowing that for all intents and purposes I would run the personnel department and being the guy that's called on to make the decisions in the draft and free agency."

The Seattle experience certainly gave Thompson a chance to spread his wings. He was the Seahawks' primary draft architect, and worked closely with general manager Bob Ferguson in overseeing all of the team's football operations.

In October 2004, when Harlan decided that Mike Sherman was spread too thin trying to handle the dual role of head coach and general manager, he consulted with Wolf and left that conversation with really just one candidate—Thompson.

"I think Ted Thompson, for a number of reasons, is the perfect fit," Harlan said the day he hired Thompson. "I had other names on that list, but I never went strongly to a second choice.

"I told Ted when I first made contact with him…that he topped my list from day one and I was going to make every attempt to do what it took to get him to Green Bay. I didn't even want to have to think about going to the second name on that list. I thought he was the one person who could come in and make this a very compatible relationship [with Sherman]."

Thompson has described himself as laid-back. But those that know him best tend to disagree.

"He comes off as laid-back," Wolf said. "But he's not laid-back. He played [10] years in the league, and he played one of the hardest positions to play.

"The toughness is there. And if you have toughness, you have confidence. He's very smart. He knows all aspects of the game, all the nuances as far as the way the league system operates. He could be a salary-cap guy, he's that smart."

While Thompson learned many things from Wolf, the two have approached the job quite differently.

Much like Thompson, Wolf was a scout at heart and that part of his job always came first.

But Wolf also loved to trade, and during his nearly 10 years running the Packers, he made a remarkable 89 trades. Wolf also loved free agency, and made several major signings, such as Reggie White, Sean Jones, Santana Dotson, and Desmond Howard.

"That's one thing I told my guys: when it's all said and done, I'm going to have two six-shooters on me and I've got 12 rounds on me," Wolf said. "And I can guarantee you fellows I'm going to fire all 12 rounds. I'm not coming back here with one revolver half full."

Thompson is also a scout first, and often spends four days a week on college campuses studying the players who will be draft eligible the following spring. Thompson takes a more conservative approach to trades and free agency, but his results over the last 11 seasons have been impressive.

The Packers have reached the postseason eight of 11 years under Thompson, including seven straight as of 2016. Green Bay has won one Super Bowl under Thompson, played in three NFC Championship Games, and won five NFC North crowns.

Part of what makes Thompson special in the way he puts together a team is the fact that he was a player. Thompson played for some very good Houston Oilers clubs in the "Love Ya Blue" era of the 1970s and early '80s.

Thompson was signed by legendary coach Bum Phillips as a lowly, undrafted free agent. He was a special teams player and backup line-backer.

Nothing was guaranteed in the NFL for players in those days, so Thompson had to make the team every year. From one of the last spots on the roster, he observed closely the locker room and how it worked—not only from an Xs and Os standpoint, but from a people perspective, as well.

This experience has served Thompson well decades later as a general manager who's in charge of putting together a team.

"The locker room is a special place," Thompson said. "Having been a player you care very deeply about it, and we're very careful who we bring into that locker room."

That doesn't mean the Packers or any other NFL team will ever put together a roster of Eagle Scouts. Every organization will take a chance on a talented player with a checkered past if they feel the talent level—and what that performer can do on the field—outweighs the risk of trouble off the field and in the locker room.

Thompson took a chance early in his tenure with wide receiver Koren Robinson, a player who was suspended for most of the 2006 season. Thompson did the same thing when he brought back defensive lineman Johnny Jolly in 2013 after his three-year suspension from the league.

Sometimes reputation belies the type of person a particular athlete might be, or how he will fit into the structure of the team—both on and off the field. Sometimes a player who has had a checkered past might actually fit into the culture of a particular team.

Let's not devalue the ability to evaluate talent. It is a huge part of this process. You have to have talented players to win, but Thompson believes in a common denominator: *Is this guy going to be a good teammate?*

During Green Bay's minicamps and training camp each summer, Thompson gets a feel for how a player will fit in.

Green Bay general manager Ted Thompson (right) has employed a draft-and-develop philosophy that's kept the Packers among the NFL's elite.

"We watch how people interact," he said.

So while outside observers focus on performance, those who see the game at a higher level also know that how a group fits in the locker room has a great deal to do with how successful they will be on the field.

Thompson believes it's the intangibles that make a successful team.

"There's a certain steadfastness to every championship team," Thompson said. "They believe in themselves and each other, even when they probably shouldn't."

That proved to be a major ingredient in Green Bay's run to a Super Bowl title in 2010. The Packers endured a season that saw 15 players land on the injured reserve list, including eight players who started at least one game that year.

There was a point that season where the remaining players who were healthy and playing might have been the only ones who believed they could still win a championship. But believe they did. And win they did, as Green Bay toppled Pittsburgh in Super Bowl XLV 31–25.

"There's a bond with good teams and that's why they're good," Thompson said.

Perhaps being mindful of the delicate relationship inside the locker room is why the Packers have used free agency judiciously under Thompson. When a free agent comes to Green Bay, Thompson must decide how he'll fit both on the field and in the locker room.

Thompson has been extremely careful who he's added to the mix. When Thompson signed Charles Woodson, a talented but somewhat mercurial star with the Oakland Raiders in 2006, many questioned the impact he would have in Green Bay.

Thompson knew his young team needed the leadership that Woodson could provide. And after a rocky start, that is exactly what Woodson gave Green Bay.

On the field, Woodson went to Pro Bowls and earned NFL Defensive Player of the Year honors in 2009. Inside the locker room, Woodson took young players like safety Nick Collins and cornerback Tramon Williams and taught them how to be professionals. Woodson showed them how to properly prepare for games, and they became Pro Bowl players partly because of his influence.

Thompson hit another home run with defensive tackle Ryan Pickett that same offseason. While Pickett didn't have quite the impact Woodson did, he was a steady, reliable starter for eight years in Green Bay.

Then, in another surprise move in 2014, Thompson signed former

Carolina and Chicago defensive end Julius Peppers, a player who became so important to his teammates that he was voted a playoff captain in 2014. That is an honor that rarely goes to a newcomer.

Just before the start of the 2007 season, Thompson sent a sixth-round draft choice to the New York Giants for running back Ryan Grant to fill an enormous void. Grant eventually gave the Packers a running game that helped them reach the NFC Championship Game that season. Along the way, Grant set the Packers' all-time, single-game post-season rushing record with 201 rushing yards and three touchdowns against Seattle in the divisional playoffs.

Observers knew the impact future Hall of Fame players like Woodson and Peppers could have on the field. Thompson knew their impact inside his locker room would be just as crucial to the success of the Packers.

Many observers and fans evaluate free-agency success based on how many players from outside the organization you sign. The Packers don't view it that way.

Green Bay is a draft-and-develop organization that brings in players and grows those players. When those players eventually reach free agency, Green Bay identifies the core players it wants to keep, and more often than not, re-signs those players to provide the foundation of the roster.

In recent seasons, the Packers used significant financial resources to keep their own talent. Quarterback Aaron Rodgers, linebacker Clay Matthews, wide receivers Jordy Nelson and Randall Cobb, and offensive tackle Bryan Bulaga head this list. More recently, defensive lineman Mike Daniels and kicker Mason Crosby were signed by the Packers prior to reaching free agency.

What Thompson and vice president of football administration/player finance Russ Ball do well is invest their resources to keep their core group intact. That's one of the reasons why they've never made much noise in free agency. If Green Bay is going to throw big money at anyone, it's usually going to be its own players.

Green Bay's conservative approach with free agency and wise invest-ments in its own stars has helped it remain in terrific shape with the NFL's salary cap. While many teams cut important players simply to get under the salary cap each year, Green Bay has had financial flexibility for years.

Draft and develop. Sign your own. Occasionally dabble in free agency.

No organization in the NFL commits to this approach quite like Green Bay.

It's the Packers Way. And Thompson & Co. are awfully good at it.

CHAPTER 8
MIKE McCARTHY

I believe the job of NFL head coach forces a person to be a leader, psychologist, dictator, demigod, taskmaster, and control freak with an unyielding "my way or the highway" approach in a perceived "us against them" world. A lot of the people who eventually become NFL head coaches have some, if not all, of these qualities in their DNA.

These characteristics are necessary because as leaders, they have to coach to the lowest common denominator of the players they work with. Remember, in the NFL there are 53 players on that roster. So sometimes that denominator can sink pretty low.

NFL coaches live in a world where one game is dissected, analyzed, and talked about for six days after its conclusion. In baseball or basketball, there are multiple games in a week. If one game doesn't go well, chances are you have another the next night. That limits dwelling on the previous game.

I've seen good people, some of whom I knew as assistants, change their entire personality and become complete jerks once they became an NFL head coach. I guess they felt they had to, because in some ways it's what the job requires.

We often talk about players having to find the "right fit," meaning the system of offense or defense that best suits their talents. I think the same is true for coaches and, in particular, head coaches in terms of fitting into the culture of an organization, town, and fandom.

It's not just about ability or capability. All of these people know their Xs and Os. It's about fit.

While I was in Kansas City, the Chiefs hired John Mackovic as their head coach in 1983. Mackovic had been an assistant in Dallas under legendary head coach Tom Landry.

Like Landry, Mackovic had a somewhat aloof, stern, but classy air about him. He appeared to be most comfortable in a coat and tie with a glass of wine in his hand. It took him four years, but he got the Chiefs back to the playoffs in 1986. He had some problems with player relations, and the Chiefs let him go after that playoff run.

Mackovic eventually ended up at Illinois, where he had a very successful tenure, leading the Illini to four straight bowl games. From there, the University of Texas came calling and Mackovic took the job.

Mackovic was a wine-and-cheese guy who liked to play golf. He was going into a steak-and-beer world where hunting was the pastime.

In an effort to make Mackovic more relatable to the Texas crowd, one year they dressed him up for a photo shoot in a cowboy hat with a gun. It didn't work. Mackovic just didn't fit the culture of Austin, and after six years, a solid 41–28–2 record, and three bowl games, he was fired.

When Ted Thompson hired Mike McCarthy to be his head coach in January 2006, he described the persona of his new coach as "Pittsburgh macho." I really believe he got it right.

Technically, McCarthy grew up in Greenfield, Pennsylvania. Greenfield is a neighborhood in Pittsburgh, a member of the 15th Ward with a population of roughly 8,000.

A trip to Greenfield is like a step back in time.

McCarthy grew up—of course—on Greenfield Avenue, a long, narrow, and winding street where everyone knows everybody else.

The houses are all made of brick and were built in the early-to-mid 1900s. Several homes have awnings; the American flag flies from most. There are some homes, too, that still have antenna ears on the roof.

The houses are so close, neighbors can high-five from their upstairs windows. The yards are small and the driveways are tight.

Life isn't easy, but there's a terrific sense of community and neighborhood pride.

"Greenfield is a place that knew me when I was developing," McCarthy said. "It is a place that made me who I am. Where I am today, I owe that to Greenfield."

McCarthy also owes plenty to his parents, Joe and Ellen. McCarthy was one of five children who grew up in an Irish Catholic house, where the prevailing themes were hard work and discipline.

Joe McCarthy was a jack-of-all-trades who worked as a fireman, a policeman, and later renovated homes—including the one Mike was raised in.

"My father's the hardest-working person I've ever been around," Mike McCarthy said. "He doesn't waste time."

Of all Joe's occupations, though, he was best known for owning Joe McCarthy's Bar & Grill. Located at the end of a hill and no bigger than most homes in Greenfield, the bar became a hangout for a neighboring steel factory that's closed today.

"The bar was packed at eight in the morning, it was packed at 4 o'clock in the afternoon, it was packed at midnight," Mike McCarthy said. "That's just the way you grew up. It's a blue-collar environment. I just think people were brought up the right way."

Mike worked in the bar each Sunday immediately after church. Mike did a little bit of everything, just like his father. He stocked the place, waited tables, tended bar, and even cleaned the bathroom in the basement.

"And Joe was harder on him than anybody else," said Bernie O'Connor, one of Mike McCarthy's 70-plus cousins. "Tough love."

The bar was then called Chasers in the Run and locals said it still looked exactly the same. There was a pool table that sat in the middle of the bar. There was a pull-lever cigarette machine. The beer was cold, the food was not for those watching their weight, and the prices might have been the lowest in America.

There were a few subtle differences, though.

The bathroom was moved upstairs. And Mike's picture—taken on the day he was hired as Green Bay's head coach—hung above a corner booth with McCarthy's signature.

To many in and around Greenfield, McCarthy has become a hero and role model.

"I am very humbled to know that, yes, maybe there is a little kid who says, 'He grew up here and he is an NFL coach, maybe I can do it someday,'" McCarthy told the *Pittsburgh Post-Gazette* in 2008. "There is a responsibility, and to hear that Pittsburgh people might look up to me is the ultimate compliment, as far as I am concerned, the ultimate compliment."

While Joe McCarthy did all he could to provide for his family, Ellen ran the house. She also worked as a secretary and part-time waitress to help keep the seven McCarthys afloat.

"I grew up the right way," Mike McCarthy said.

Baseball was always McCarthy's best sport, and he was such a prolific hitter, opposing teams would walk him with the bases loaded. McCarthy was also a terrific leader and tenacious basketball player.

On the football field, McCarthy was a defensive end, a tight end, a kicker, and a punter. Football was probably his third-best sport, though, and few would have predicted it would one day become his meal ticket.

But Baker University, an NAIA school in Baldwin City, Kansas, offered McCarthy a chance to play college football and continue chasing his dreams. It was there that McCarthy blossomed into a standout tight end and a captain, and recently was inducted into that school's Hall of Fame.

"To have a Baker University athletic alumnus make it to the pinnacle of coaching as a head coach of an NFL team is just unimaginable," said Baker athletic director Dan Harris, who was an assistant football coach for the Wildcats in the mid-1980s when McCarthy played at Baker. "Mike has created a new level of respectability for a traditional powerhouse NFL football program."

After graduating from Baker with a business administration degree, McCarthy landed a graduate assistant job at Fort Hayes State, where he coached linebackers in 1987 and '88. One of McCarthy's big coaching breaks, though, came in 1989, when University of Pittsburgh coach Paul Hackett hired him as a volunteer assistant.

McCarthy wasn't paid initially. But the staff he worked on included Marvin Lewis and Jon Gruden, who would both go on to become NFL head coaches. And McCarthy and Hackett forged a terrific bond.

Perhaps the most important thing McCarthy was exposed to at Pitt was the West Coast offense. Hackett had learned the offense from its master, former San Francisco 49ers coach Bill Walsh. And while McCarthy would later put his own stamp on it, the West Coast offense became his staple.

Hackett was fired after the 1992 season, but landed the offensive coordinator job with the Kansas City Chiefs. Much to McCarthy's delight, Hackett—and Chiefs head coach Marty Schottenheimer—brought McCarthy along as an offensive assistant/quality control coach.

McCarthy was giddy. He was just 29 years old and had already achieved one dream of working in the NFL.

McCarthy studied Schottenheimer's every move. And McCarthy has referred to him countless times since coming to Green Bay.

"I'm very grateful to Marty Schottenheimer," McCarthy said. "He gave me my first opportunity in the league. I have great respect for him on a personal and professional level."

McCarthy spent six years with the Chiefs, the last four as their quarterbacks coach. In that time, he worked with Hall of Fame Player Joe Montana, future MVP Rich Gannon, and solid pros Elvis Grbac and Steve Bono.

It was also in Kansas City that McCarthy started believing he could become an NFL head coach one day.

"Having the opportunity to be around Marty Schottenheimer and just the way he ran his program, his work ethic," McCarthy said. "I felt as an assistant coach that that's when it came to me that I felt that I'd be able to be a head coach in this league someday. I couldn't tell you an exact date, but it was at some point in my career in Kansas City."

Green Bay hired McCarthy as its quarterbacks coach in 1999, and he jumped at the opportunity to work with Brett Favre. But Packers head coach Ray Rhodes was fired after just one year, and McCarthy was on the move again.

The Rhodes debacle didn't hurt McCarthy's stock, as New Orleans hired him to be its offensive coordinator. But there was nothing easy about landing that job.

McCarthy laughs today about preparing his résumé for three days at a Kinko's on Oneida Street in Green Bay. McCarthy then spent the better part of a week interviewing for the position with head coach Jim Haslett and assistant head coach Rick Venturi.

"We went to the office the first day and then every night about 10:00, 11:00, Jim Haslett and Rick Venturi, we would just start talking about football, different situations, different circumstances," McCarthy remembers. "And after about five days it was, I mean, it got to be monotonous. It was like, you asked me that question three times already.

"We were at dinner with [quarterback] Jeff Blake. We just signed Jeff Blake with a free-agent contract, and Jim said, 'You need to talk to him about what you're going to do on offense.' I said, 'Well, I don't even know where we are.' He goes, 'Oh, hell, you got the job. You knew that, didn't you?' That's how I found out I had it. Good experience."

So was McCarthy's time in New Orleans.

Over the next five seasons, the Saints set 10 offensive team records and 25 individual marks, and enjoyed the most explosive stretch in the franchise's 40-year history. McCarthy was named the NFL's Assistant Coach of the Year in 2000 and helped the Saints rank as the No. 1 scoring offense in football in 2002.

McCarthy became San Francisco's offensive coordinator in 2005, but the 49ers struggled immensely on offense and finished 32nd in football. San Francisco was decimated by injuries that season. And rookie quarterback Alex Smith—the No. 1 pick in that April's draft—wasn't ready to play.

It all added up to a 4–12 season for the 49ers. Despite the disappointing year, McCarthy's stock remained high.

When the Green Bay Packers dumped Mike Sherman after the 2005 season, McCarthy applied. But most considered him a long shot—at best.

Packers general manager Ted Thompson would eventually interview seven candidates. Some were surprised McCarthy made it even that far.

Thompson met with Dallas assistant head coach/passing game coordinator Sean Payton, Cleveland offensive coordinator Maurice Carthon, Chicago defensive coordinator Ron Rivera, McCarthy, San Diego defensive coordinator Wade Phillips, New York Giants defensive coordinator Tim Lewis, and Packers defensive coordinator Jim Bates.

Of those, Payton was the young, hot assistant coach at the time. And many believed he was the favorite.

The extremely cerebral and methodical Thompson took his time. He always does.

And 10 days after Thompson fired Sherman, he made the surprising decision to hire McCarthy.

"I don't think there was any one," Thompson said of the factors that led him to McCarthy. "I think it was just the whole. I tried to obviously focus on the small things and the things I thought were really, really important.

"I had these long sheets of paper that I'd go through and I'd scribble and at the end of it I always had reminder things. And I talked to a lot of different people and I'd say, 'What makes a good head coach, what makes a good working relationship?' Those kind of things."

One thing that certainly has made the McCarthy–Green Bay marriage work is fit. McCarthy fits Green Bay and Green Bay fits McCarthy. That fit is one reason McCarthy's hire has worked out so well for both sides.

McCarthy is one of the more complete people I have seen in the job of head coach. He has a good feel for work, play, and family. McCarthy also has perspective on where life fits in the all-encompassing world of directing an NFL football team. The fact that life fits at all in this job separates him from most NFL head coaches I have known.

For example, in 2011, the Packers were scheduled to play the Chicago Bears at Lambeau Field on the night of December 25. Even before a home game, NFL teams stay in a hotel. This allows the team to meet one last time before game day and gives the coaching staff a little more control over the players, making sure everyone completes their final preparations and gets their sleep.

But on this date, for this game, McCarthy allowed his players and coaches to spend Christmas Eve and Christmas morning at home with their families. I can't think of another NFL head coach who would have made that kind of accommodation on the night before a game. By the way, the Packers had their usual night before the game meeting on Christmas afternoon, then went out and beat the Bears that night 35–21.

"I think he's got great balance in a lot of areas," said Joe Philbin, who was McCarthy's offensive line coach in 2006 and his offensive coordinator from 2007 to 2011. "His perspective is excellent. He's gotten very passionate about things that are important to him. I think that's clearly evident. And he's got balance, balance with the staff, balance with the players.

"He knows when to be tough, when to lighten up. He's got a good feel for those types of things, both with his coaching staff and his team. I think that's a real strength of his. And I think he's got a passion that the staff feels as well. The passion to achieve something special and honor the tradition and build on it and that's good. Those are two real good qualities that he has.

"He's very poised and I think that's part of the balance he has in football and out of football. That's certainly different. We all hope you evolve and grow as a coach. Maybe he's a little bit more poised than he was earlier. I don't care how prepared you are, I'm guessing when you become a head coach there's pressures you weren't sure of and probably until you sit in that chair you're not too certain about it. And so as he sat in that chair longer, I think he's gotten a good, wider perspective on things and he's been able to deal with the ups and downs really well."

Defensive coordinator Dom Capers, a former head coach in both Carolina and Houston, agrees.

"I think Mike's very consistent," Capers said. "I think he's had a plan since he's been here and a vision of what he wants this team to look like. This is a business that's a roller-coaster business and we're all evaluated on what we do right now. What we did yesterday really has no relevance.

"So I think being able to be consistent with that message and be demanding and consistent in terms of the effort and the focus, in the meeting room and practice field and weight room and everything you do, you create a culture that's just standing operating procedure in the way we do business. And that benefits you in the long haul."

Former Marquette and current Indiana men's basketball coach Tom Crean has a unique insight into coaching, and in particular, football coaches. Crean married into a family of football coaches.

Crean's father-in-law is former college head coach Jack Harbaugh. Both of his brothers-in-law are football coaches, too. John is the head coach of the Baltimore Ravens, while Jim is the head coach at Michigan and coached the San Francisco 49ers for four seasons.

So it was no surprise that Crean and McCarthy struck up a good friendship while they were both working high-profile coaching jobs in Wisconsin. McCarthy is a basketball fan, in particular college basketball.

I met Crean long before he got to Marquette, while he was an assistant at Michigan State. We had a nice, friendly relationship through my visits to East Lansing on the Big Ten basketball trail.

Crean and McCarthy share one common trait: a tremendous passion for their professions. About a year after the Packers hired McCarthy, I had a conversation with Crean and he mentioned that "Mike has a great feel for people, his players especially, and that's what makes him a great coach." Crean could not have been any more on point.

Communication and consistency are two enormous positives I've

Creativity, drive, and a feel for his players have helped Mike McCarthy become one of the top coaches in the NFL.

seen from McCarthy. They are foundations in what he does, and why he's had tremendous success since becoming a surprising hire as Green Bay's head coach back in 2006.

"I think it's important to stay in the structure of my position and just be a consistent individual," McCarthy said. "I don't try to be liked. I don't try to be disliked either. Because at the end of the day, being a head coach, it's lonely sometimes because you have to keep your eye on the target and be in tune with what's going on with the culture and structure. You don't have the time to maybe have that relationship that you did as an assistant coach or even a coordinator. And I miss all that.

"But to me, communication is the key to everything. I believe first and foremost communication is a two-way street. I've learned so much in life and coaching, not by talking but by listening. I think that's very important to practice what you preach.

"And I've talked about communication since the day I got into coaching. It's nothing that's new to any relationship that I've been a part of in the National Football League. Hopefully it's working."

It is.

McCarthy is one of the best play callers I have seen on the NFL level. He can match Xs and Os with the best of them. But I believe his finest quality is his feel for people and in particular his players.

Although McCarthy's office is on the third floor inside Lambeau Field, he'll spend much of his time on the first floor, where the weight room, locker room, and training room are.

"It's the old bartender theory," McCarthy said. "You've got to be down there amongst them. The No. 1 responsibility I have as the head coach of the Green Bay Packers is I have to keep my finger on the pulse of the football team.

"That's how you make better decisions. And if you're not in tune to what's going on with the people that you're responsible for, your decision-making is going to be affected."

It is my observation that McCarthy doesn't handle *players*. He leads *people*. There is a big difference in the two.

Players aren't machines or commodities. They are flesh and blood with spirit and feelings. McCarthy understands the psyche of the athlete and the challenges an athlete faces. The most successful coaches on the professional level don't just have good talent on their rosters to coach. The best coaches know how to fit talented people together.

"I've seen him get mad…but sometimes he's just really fired up, too," said former Packers defensive tackle Ryan Pickett. "Coach has a lot of fire in him, and he gets the best out of us, but at the same time it's respect.

"That's why players love him. You won't find one player on this team that doesn't love playing for him. Everybody. He's just that kind of coach."

Thompson, who made the surprise move of hiring McCarthy, agreed.

"He does a very good job of being organized," Thompson said of McCarthy. "He does a very good job of handling the chaos coming from the job and he keeps a fairly even keel. I like all those things. I think those are good qualities."

With successful coaches there is no such thing as "my way or the highway," even with Vince Lombardi. Jerry Kramer, in his 1968 book *Instant Replay*, recalls how even a stern taskmaster like Lombardi knew whom to push, whom to pat on the back and when to do it.

That old line "He treats us all the same—like dogs" must have been said in jest by Packers Hall of Fame defensive tackle Henry Jordan because it simply was not true of Lombardi.

I've observed McCarthy up close since he was hired in January 2006. I don't believe the Packers would have gotten to the playoffs or won Super Bowl XLV without McCarthy's feel for his players that season.

"He's not one of these guys that says, 'I don't care what you say. We're doing it my way,'" said former Packers safety Charlie Peprah. "He listens to his guys and will change if it benefits the team."

Late in that 2010 season, with a number of players lost to injury, McCarthy knew he needed to inject confidence in those who were still healthy enough to play. He used actions and words to instill confidence in a team at its lowest ebb.

It was December 15, 2010, and the Packers were in crisis mode.

Green Bay had just lost in Detroit 7–3 in arguably its worst performance of McCarthy's five-year tenure. The loss left the Packers at 8–5—two games behind NFC North–leading Chicago, and in a fight for their playoff lives.

Aaron Rodgers, who left the Lions game with a concussion late in the second quarter, was listed as doubtful the following week. Deep down, though, McCarthy knew he wouldn't have Rodgers, a player who had quickly developed into one of football's elite signal callers.

To top it off, Green Bay was facing its toughest test of the year, a Sunday night road tilt at AFC power New England. The Patriots entered the contest having won 10 of 11 games, had the NFL's soon-to-be MVP in quarterback Tom Brady, and were averaging a league-high 31.9 points per game.

McCarthy was also facing growing concerns from the paying customers. In the nearly three seasons since Brett Favre had been traded, the Packers were 25–20 and hadn't won a single playoff game.

In many places, that record would be just fine. But in the NFL's smallest city—affectionately known as Titletown thanks to its 13 World Championships—McCarthy and his program were at a fork in the road.

Now, all McCarthy had to do was go into New England without his best player and face football's finest team. To the oddsmakers, who installed the Patriots as 14-point favorites, the Packers were entering a gun fight with only a few pebbles.

Not to McCarthy.

For five years, McCarthy had been cooperative each time he met with the local media. McCarthy was always extremely positive, using that word so often that many referred to him as Mike McPositive.

McCarthy aimed to find the good in most situations, which meant he rarely made headlines with his words. His answers were sometimes generic. He was guarded, protective, cautious.

But on this Wednesday afternoon, four days before Green Bay met the Patriots, McCarthy dramatically changed his approach. Instead of dishing out vanilla, McCarthy went for a scoop of Cherry Garcia.

And everyone took notice.

"We're nobody's underdog," McCarthy bellowed when he was asked about facing the mighty New England Patriots. "We have all the confidence in our abilities. We've had challenges throughout the season. We've stepped up to those challenges, and we feel the same way going into this game."

Four nights later, the Packers met almost every challenge that came their way. Almost.

McCarthy, continuing his bold, new approach, deferred after the Packers won the opening toss. Then McCarthy opened the game with an onside kick, which the Packers recovered.

Backup quarterback Matt Flynn threw for three touchdowns and 251 yards. The Packers held the high-powered Patriots to 249 total yards and had nearly twice as many first downs as New England.

But a pair of critical Green Bay turnovers and some special teams breakdowns allowed New England to escape with a 31–27 win. Afterward, though, something had changed inside Green Bay's locker room.

There was a restored confidence. There was a belief and a certainty that had been missing for weeks now.

The Packers entered 2010 talking about a Super Bowl title, but had disappointed many with a 3–3 start and an 8–5 record heading to New England. But McCarthy's "nobody's underdog" comment seemed to re-energize and rally his team—even though the mighty Patriots prevailed that night.

"There's no doubt about it," Pickett said. "New England wasn't just a good team, they were a great team. And when coach called us 'nobody's underdogs,' it seemed to fire everybody up a little bit.

"If guys kind of needed a jolt, that was it. We knew we had a great team, but I know people were starting to doubt us, too. I guess it was time to show we weren't anybody's underdog and that's what we went and did."

Packers right guard Josh Sitton agreed.

"I think that New England game was definitely a turning point," Sitton said. "Obviously our goal is to go out and win every game, but we went and proved to them we can go frickin' play with anybody. I definitely think that was a turning point."

The Packers had a renewed sense of confidence, thanks in part to the actions of their head coach, who showed an unwavering belief in them. Later that postseason, McCarthy pulled another stunner.

On Saturday night, less than 24 hours before Super Bowl XLV, McCarthy made the bold move of fitting his players for the championship rings. Traditionally, teams get fitted after winning a title. But the McCarthy Way was now much different than many of his peers.

"I felt the measurement of the rings—the timing of it would be special," McCarthy said. "It would have a significant effect on our players doing it the night before the game.

"I just told them, 'We're going to get measured for rings tonight.' Scheduling is so important during the course of the week. You want to do certain things at certain times. I thought that was a perfect time. I thought it would be special and give us a boost of confidence to do it the night before the game."

The Packers' confidence was sky high. And it was a big reason Green Bay defeated Pittsburgh 31–25 in the 45th Super Bowl the following night.

"That's pretty how much he coached us all year, and especially at the end," Pickett said. "He had a lot of confidence in us and we had a lot of confidence in each other."

Former cornerback Charles Woodson agreed.

"No matter what anyone said about him he never changed his focus on getting to this point," Woodson said of McCarthy. "When you have a coach who is unwavered by whatever is going on in the media or whatever is said about him, you know that you have a good guy at the helm."

McCarthy's feel for his players is similar to what I saw in the greatest coach I have ever been around, the NBA's Phil Jackson.

Jackson won 11 NBA championships—six of them in Chicago, where I covered him while he was with the Chicago Bulls. The secret to Jackson was his feel for people, not Xs and Os. Not the triangle offense. Not all this other BS. His genius was his understanding and feel for people.

In 1992, the Bulls were playing the Portland Trail Blazers in the NBA Finals. The first two games were in Chicago, and the Bulls lost the second game on a Friday night. Now the series was tied 1–1, and Portland had all the momentum in the world. Chicago was heading to Portland the next day for a Sunday Game 3. It was a really short turn-around for going one city to the next.

When we got on the plane, Jackson told the guys to take a break—they weren't going to practice that day. He told them to just get focused spiritually and mentally, and they'd have a shootaround the day of the game. Then they went out and they kicked Portland's ass and that Game 3 turned around that whole series. That was Phil Jackson just understanding that his team was really tired. They didn't want to jump on a plane after Game 2, fly to Portland, and practice.

But 99 percent of the coaches I know would have practiced their team on that Saturday. They would have flown out there right after the game, arrived early, gone through a two-hour practice, and then tried to play the next night.

But Jackson won 11 titles because he knows people, he knows how players are feeling, he understands the spirituality of the whole situation—and there is spirituality in pro sports. It's very much the spirit of the team and the player—how they feel and where they are—and Jackson understood that.

And I think Mike McCarthy understands that, as well. Jackson and McCarthy share the trait of flexibility, another quality that sets them apart from the rest.

Mike McCarthy understands people. He knows when to back off and when to press hard. And it's because he understands that maybe he can't push his guys past a certain point one day. He'll save it for tomorrow. I think that's part of what makes him so good.

"Mike is a guy [who] has a great balance," former linebacker Brady Poppinga said. "He's intense when he has to be, but he's also relaxed."

I think McCarthy is a great play caller, a brilliant offensive mind. But I think the success that he's attained is due to his skills with people. I don't think the Packers go to the Super Bowl in 2010 without that element of Mike McCarthy. They don't get there. That was a wonderful run, but the gist of what happened took place behind the scenes.

I do think that run was Mike's genius and his feel for people and what to do and how to restore confidence in his team. He had 15 players and eight preferred starters on the injured reserve list.

That team by December, after their loss in Detroit, didn't think they were good enough. I know they didn't. You'll never get them to admit that, but you could just tell. It was like, *Well, we have all of these injuries. It's just not our year.* Athletes can slip into that, but McCarthy's actions really boosted their confidence down the stretch.

The players do read the papers, no matter what they might tell you. And how a coach handles a team in the media is extremely important. When McCarthy went to the team before the New England game, he told them they weren't going to have Aaron Rodgers. But he also made his comment about the team being "nobody's underdog."

Then he said, "If we win the toss, we're going to defer," and everybody wondered why they would do that. Then he said "We're going to onside kick, we're going to recover it, and we're going to score. Then we're going to dictate the momentum of the game the entire night."

And, by God, they did.

That team lost the game—and they lost on a special teams snafu. But the Packers, with Matt Flynn at quarterback, played really, really well. And I remember coming back on the plane you could just feel the renewed confidence.

The next week, before the Packers played the New York Giants, Aaron Rodgers said to me, "You know, it was good I got a week off because I feel great now. I feel rejuvenated." And Rodgers started playing great after that. He was lights-out. And they kicked the Giants that day 45–17.

In one of the biggest games of Rodgers' first three years as a starter, he had arguably his finest performance. Rodgers threw for a career-high 404 yards, tied a personal best with four touchdown passes, and posted the third-highest passer rating of his career (139.9).

Rodgers, who was still looking for a signature win, got it against the Giants. The result was a stunning rout of the Giants that had the Packers back in control of their playoff destiny.

The Packers (9–6) moved into sixth place in the NFC playoff race. The Giants (9–6) fell into seventh place.

"It was fun," Rodgers said at the time. "I had a good week of preparation this week. I think that's kind of where it started. I felt good throwing the ball all week, liked the game plan, liked the things we were trying to do and once we were into the game, I liked the rhythm that Mike [McCarthy] had our offense in."

One game remained, a must-win that would save or sink Green Bay's season.

The Packers prepared to host bitter rival Chicago, a team with nothing to play for. But really, that didn't matter.

The Bears had wrapped up the NFC North division title, and by kickoff they were locked in as the No. 2 seed in the conference. All week long, though, former Chicago head coach Lovie Smith insisted he would play his starters.

Instead of worrying about the Bears, the Packers focused on themselves. Good thing, too.

To the surprise of many, Chicago played its starters the entire game, trying to keep McCarthy's Packers out of the postseason. But Green Bay's defense was sensational and the Packers posted a 10–3 win, earning the sixth and final playoff spot.

When Smith and McCarthy met at the 50-yard line after the game, McCarthy said to him, "Congratulations on the division title." And Lovie said, "Nice win today. We'll see you in a few weeks."

And Smith was exactly right. He knew. And that's why he didn't want any part of the Packers.

"I kept thinking we're going to see them again," Bears cornerback Tim Jennings said of the Packers. "I was thinking, 'Man, we should have knocked them out.'"

Instead, the Packers knocked the Bears out three weeks later when Green Bay posted a 21–14 win in the NFC Championship Game.

That set the stage for the Packers to capture Super Bowl XLV and for McCarthy to make good on a promise he made during his initial press conference in Green Bay.

"I'd like to acknowledge the fans of Green Bay and just to let you know that there will be an unconditional commitment from Ted and myself to bring a World Championship back to Green Bay," McCarthy said that day. "I think that's very important to state that right up front."

McCarthy delivered.

When I think about that 2010 Super Bowl team, I think McCarthy got a lot of guys to step up and play better than they ever have before. That team would have never won for someone like Mike Sherman. But they won for McCarthy.

Just think of the guys on the sideline that year—Jermichael Finley, Ryan Grant, Nick Barnett, Mark Tauscher. And amazingly, a lot of the guys who filled in that year were better than the guys they replaced, except at tight end. They couldn't replace Jermichael Finley, and they still haven't to this day.

McCarthy instilled confidence in that team. McCarthy not only said he believed in them, he showed them by the way he handled things. By the time they got to the playoffs, they were an extremely confident bunch.

"I did some things that were different, but frankly, just trust your instincts," McCarthy said of how he handled the 2010 season. "I think the No. 1 responsibility as the head coach is to have your finger on the pulse of your football team and react and respond accordingly. That's what I felt myself and our coaching staff did. We stayed true to our operation. We didn't change the way we prepare for games, we didn't change the way we practice.

"I am not perfect, but the one thing I think the players truly know that they get from me, they get the truth and it comes from the heart. They know it is researched. They know our staff is very detail oriented. We don't ever walk into a meeting unprepared.

"There is a belief in how we operate and I think that was the biggest key for us down the stretch. I just felt we were a consistent football team all year. I never felt we were as bad as our record may have been some time or as good when we had the blowout win. I felt we were just a very consistent football team and I think that is why we ended up being the Super Bowl champions."

What I like about McCarthy is his insatiable thirst for doing something better. McCarthy is always willing to make changes. He's a very intelligent guy.

Every year McCarthy analyzes his entire program and every year there are adjustments. Some work; some don't. But McCarthy does not have that "my way or the highway" mentality. If the highway doesn't lead to the promised land, then he gets off that road and onto another.

McCarthy is not afraid to fail and thus is not afraid to step out of his comfort zone. McCarthy has reconfigured his coaching staff several times.

McCarthy gave up game-day play calling and changed the roles of several assistant coaches following Green Bay's devastating loss in the NFC Championship game at Seattle to end the 2014 season. But when those changes didn't work out as well as McCarthy had hoped during a frustrating 2015 season, he took back the play-calling card, then adjusted his staff heading into the 2016 season.

"The personal part of it was brutal," McCarthy said of taking play-calling duties back from Tom Clements. "Professionally, I felt like I had to do it. I was worried about making sure I was going to do my job good, like I do every day. A lot of extra preparation and had a lot of help from the staff like we always do.

"We have a pretty good process of putting together game plans and getting our players ready to play. We've done it at a very high level for 10 years here, and once again we made an adjustment and that's the way we'll go."

There is a belief in coaching, that after a certain amount of time the coach has to move on because his message gets stale in the locker room. That certainly may have been the case years ago.

But with free agency today, players are coming and going every year. So the shelf life of an NFL coach might be a little longer these days.

McCarthy has a great ability to freshen his message every year. That is a tribute to his feel for his players and his flexibility.

Thus after a decade on the job his leadership still resonates in his locker room.

CHAPTER 9
THE BLESSED SEASON

One of my favorite seasons came in 2007, when Green Bay made a surprising run to the NFC Championship Game.

The Packers began the 2006 campaign just 1–4 and were 4–8 late in the year. But Green Bay finished that season with four straight wins, improved to 8–8, and carried some momentum into the 2007 season.

Still, expectations were modest—at best—for the 2007 Packers.

Despite the Packers' strong finish, general manager Ted Thompson was entering just his third season of rebuilding Green Bay's roster. It was the first time I saw something in Mike McCarthy that led me to believe he had a chance to become a great head coach.

The Packers were still the youngest team in the NFL, but McCarthy did a great job of making sure the strong finish to the 2006 campaign carried over into the offseason program, training camp, and what was soon to become a blessed 2007 for the Green and Gold.

That is not easy to do in today's era of player movement. Before free agency, teams could go from one season to another virtually intact. You could carry momentum from one season to the next.

For example, in 1984, the surprising Chicago Bears made it to the NFC Championship game, where they were shut out by the San Francisco 49ers 23–0. That game galvanized those Bears during the off-season, and they came into the 1985 campaign with an edge that helped them dominate that year.

Green Bay, led by veteran quarterback Brett Favre, won four straight games to open the 2007 campaign. The Packers defeated Philadelphia 16–13 in Week 1 on rookie kicker Mason Crosby's last-second game-winning field goal. Green Bay rolled past the New York Giants 35–13 in Week 2, and defeated highly regarded San Diego 31–24 the following week.

It was that victory over the Chargers that started to make me a believer that this very young Packers team could be on to something. They went blow-for-blow with Philip Rivers and one of the top teams in the AFC that afternoon, and I think that game fueled a belief in those Packers as well.

Then in Week 4, Green Bay downed Minnesota 23–16 in the Metrodome. In that game, Favre broke Dan Marino's record for career touchdown passes when he zipped No. 421 to Greg Jennings.

"I mean his experience, the ability to get the ball out of his hand and the urgency and accuracy that he's throwing the football with, that's what makes Brett Favre Brett Favre," McCarthy said. "He can make the tight throws, and he's just doing an excellent job managing the game, and letting our playmakers make plays."

Favre would also pass Marino later that season and become the NFL's all-time leader in career passing yards, passing attempts, and completions.

"I've said this all along and will continue to say it, I've never considered myself in the same league as Dan Marino," Favre said that season. "What a great passer, maybe the greatest passer ever.

"The way he did it is probably the way you would coach another guy to do it. The way I've done it, I don't know if you would coach guys to do it that way. But it's worked for me, and to be mentioned in the same breath with him is quite an honor."

Green Bay fell to 4–1 after a home loss to the defending NFC Champion Chicago Bears. But the Packers won their next six games, including a dramatic Monday-night victory at Denver when Favre hit Greg Jennings on an 82-yard touchdown pass on the first play of overtime for a 19–13 win.

Green Bay went to Dallas in late November to face a Cowboys team that was also 10–1. It marked just the eighth time in NFL history two teams with 10–1 records—or better—had met.

On many fronts, the night was a disaster for the Packers. Favre struggled miserably, threw two early interceptions, then exited with an elbow injury and the Packers in a 27–10 hole.

Over the next two-plus hours, though, No. 2 quarterback Aaron Rodgers showed there might indeed be life after Favre.

Rodgers finished the game 18-of-26 for 201 yards, threw his first NFL touchdown pass, and posted an impressive passer rating of 104.8.

Yet Green Bay never could get over the hump and fell 37–27 in a game that eventually gave the Cowboys the NFC's No. 1 seed. But Rodgers won a lot of people over with his performance that night.

"I just can't say enough about his preparation, because I didn't even blink," McCarthy said of Rodgers. "I didn't throw anything out.

"I've been in that position before when you have to go to your backup or go to your third guy or even your fourth guy. I went through it in San Francisco, and you just start crossing plays off the chart, and that wasn't the case. I thought Aaron did an excellent job."

Even Favre sang Rodgers' praises afterward.

"I thought he played great," Favre said that night of Rodgers. "Gave us a chance to win. I thought he was ready to play. I was hoping it would be in different circumstances…but I thought he did a fine job."

General manager Ted Thompson, the man who had drafted Rodgers and had yet to receive a return on his investment, was also quite giddy.

"I'm not trying to be glib, but I've liked him all along," Thompson said of Rodgers. "Yeah, he went through some tough times, but pre-season games and that sort of thing, and even the [New England] game he played in [2006], I don't think necessarily is the telling tale.

"I think he's a young man that's confident, that's smart, that is physically talented, that believes he can play, and has understood and accepted the role that he's in, even though he still wants to play. I'm proud of the way he carries himself. I think he's going to be a good player, and I'm pleased with the way he's playing now."

Favre returned to the lineup 10 days later, and the Packers won their next two games and clinched the NFC North Division title. Green Bay was rolling offensively behind Favre, McCarthy, and wide receivers Donald Driver and Jennings. That collection of talent and coaching helped Green Bay field one of the best passing offenses in the league.

Perhaps Favre didn't like to be coached hard, but he produced when held accountable and had one of the better seasons of his career. Favre threw for 4,155 yards, 28 touchdowns, and 15 interceptions in 2007, and his passer rating of 95.7 was the third best of his career. McCarthy was coaching Favre hard, and the three-time MVP quarterback was responding.

The Packers thrived in good weather and also went 3–0 inside domes, scoring 30 or more points in nine of their 16 games. Under McCarthy, Green Bay had become a great dome team. They were a skilled, almost finesse offensive group that was at its best when the conditions were ideal.

But when the Packers traveled to Chicago for a rematch with the Bears, they were in anything but a dome. That December Sunday, Green Bay faced 16-degree temperatures and a brutal wind. We used to call that wind "the Hawk" off Lake Michigan, and that day, it sunk the wind chill to minus-18.

It was a bone-chilling day and Favre, one of the best bad-weather quarterbacks in NFL history, wanted nothing to do with the miserable conditions by the lakefront. That young Green Bay team followed the lead of its veteran quarterback that season—who else were they going to look up to?—and with Favre in the tank, the Packers were routed 35–7.

How bad was Favre? He threw two interceptions—including one that linebacker Brian Urlacher returned for a touchdown—and had a passer rating of just 40.2 that day.

For Chicago, it was a sweep of the season series with Green Bay, the only feather in the Bears' cap in a 7–9 season. Favre's disdain for weather would come into play a few weeks later, but the Packers did finish the regular season with a 34–13 victory over Detroit to cap an improbable 13–3 regular season and earn the NFC's No. 2 seed in the upcoming playoffs.

Following a bye week, the Packers welcomed a veteran Seattle team to Lambeau Field for the NFC Divisional playoffs. The Seahawks had much of the same team that advanced to the Super Bowl in 2005 and felt good about their chances to make a deep playoff run.

It was a late-afternoon game on Saturday, January 12. The NFL's youngest team was shaky at the outset. Ryan Grant fumbled on Green Bay's first two offensive possessions, and the veteran Seahawks converted both for touchdowns and a quick 14–0 lead.

Shortly thereafter, it began to snow and Green Bay began to play. The Packers scored touchdowns on their next six possessions and blew out the Seahawks 42–20.

Grant overcame those two early fumbles and set a new franchise postseason rushing record with 201 yards. Grant's rushing mark was the seventh-highest in NFL postseason history, and for good measure, he scored three touchdowns.

"It's unfortunate what happened," Grant said of the two early fumbles. "But I really appreciate everybody backing me. They backed me the whole time.

"From the training staff to the coaches to the players, everybody just said, 'Stay with it. You know what you've got to do. Let it go.'"

The contest also became known as the "Snow Globe" game.

Snow fell throughout the game on a playable 31-degree early evening in a quintessential Lambeau playoff setting. If the great artist Norman Rockwell were still alive, he would have painted that game in that stadium.

I remember calling my wife, Julie, at halftime because I was concerned about how bad the weather was in southeast Wisconsin. I had to make a flight out of Milwaukee to Atlanta the next day to join the Chicago Bulls, whose games I was working on WGN-TV.

Julie said the weather was fine, and as I found out later, the snow dissipated in Manitowoc, 30 miles south of Green Bay.

It was almost like Green Bay was in a snow globe. The snow was seemingly only for Green Bay, the Packers, a national television audience, and football fans everywhere. It was the kind of setting that puts Lambeau

Field on the bucket lists of many, whether they are Packers fans or not.

In all, the Packers couldn't have had much more fun in the snow.

With the game well in hand late, Favre made a snowball and drilled wideout Donald Driver in the back. Driver later retaliated with a snowball to Favre's head.

"I hit Donald with a snowball. I did," Favre said. "When I kind of packed it up and threw it, it got kind of hard, like a golf ball. So I kind of threw it at his back or his butt or something.

"I'm thinking, 'You don't want to puncture an eye or something.' He turns around, packs one, and hits me in the face. Good thing it hit my facemask; it might have hit my tooth or something."

Unfortunately for Green Bay, that fun would end one week later.

Green Bay hosted the New York Giants in the NFC Championship Game, and entered the contest a 7.5-point favorite. Packer Nation was already making its Super Bowl plans.

Forecasts called for subzero temperatures in northeast Wisconsin, though, and Favre and the offensive unit wanted no part of those conditions. They all remembered what had happened in Chicago a month ago. The "old gunslinger" wasn't what he used to be in nasty weather—certainly when that weather bordered on arctic.

For me, this was my first championship game broadcast with the Packers and only the second of my career. It was a matchup of two great rivals whose playoff history was steeped in NFL tradition.

Vince Lombardi's first two NFL titles came at the expense of the Giants in the early 1960s. Neither team was expected to be in this game, so both felt like they were destiny's darlings, and with good reason. The Packers were 14–3 and playing at home, but the Giants were on a roll with road wins at Tampa Bay and Dallas during their improbable playoff run.

The weather lived up to its billing. It was minus-3 degrees at kickoff, with winds at 12 miles per hour and humidity at 49 percent. It was too cold to snow, and it only got colder as the night ensued.

Giants coach Tom Coughlin's face turned eight shades of purple and the explosive Packers offense that had produced 42 points and 408 yards the week before against Seattle was frozen right from the outset.

One play in the first half illustrated the difference in these two teams on that night. New York running back Brandon Jacobs bowled over Packers All-Pro cornerback Charles Woodson on a run with a vicious display of brute force! That play, more than any other in the entire game, illustrated the Giants' physical advantage.

It felt like the Giants were dominating the game, but they led just 6–0 on a pair of Lawrence Tynes field goals when the Packers made the play of the half. On first-and-10 from the Green Bay 10-yard line, cornerback Corey Webster fell down covering Donald Driver on the right sideline. Favre lofted a pass to "Double-D," who went 90 yards to the north end zone, tying the game. It is the longest pass in the Packers' long postseason history.

Mason Crosby later added a 36-yard field goal to give the Packers a 10–6 halftime advantage.

The Giants used their force to score rushing touchdowns by Jacobs and Ahmad Bradshaw in the third quarter. In between, Favre hit tight end Donald Lee with a 12-yard touchdown pass, then a Crosby field goal tied the game with 11:46 remaining.

The Giants were dominating the game, though, with 81 offensive plays to just 49 for Green Bay. Twice, New York drove into field-goal range. But Tynes missed from 43 yards and later 36 yards on the final play of regulation.

Tied at 20, the teams went to overtime on the coldest night of that NFL season. In OT, Favre locked on to Driver, and Webster jumped the route and gave New York the football in Green Bay territory.

The Giants eventually turned the game over to Tynes once again, and this time his 47-yard field goal sent New York to Super Bowl XLII. Two weeks later, those Giants stunned the 18–0 New England Patriots in one of the greatest upsets in Super Bowl history.

"In some ways, it was a surprise to a lot of people we were in this game," Favre said. "Unfortunately, the last thing you remember usually is a game like tonight. For me, the last play. But there have been so many great achievements that will stand out."

For the Packers, the Blessed Season was over. So was Favre's Green Bay career.

Most expected Favre to return to Green Bay for the 2008 season. Instead, on March 4, 2008, Favre said he didn't have "anything left to give" and retired.

"I know I can still play, but it's like I told my wife, I'm just tired mentally. I'm just tired," Favre said. "If I felt like coming back...the only way for me to be successful would be to win a Super Bowl. To go to the Super Bowl and lose, would almost be worse than anything else. Anything less than a Super Bowl win would be unsuccessful.

"I know it shouldn't feel unsuccessful, but the only way to come back and make that be the right decision would be to come back and win a Super Bowl and honestly the odds of that, they're tough. Those are big shoes for me to fill, and I guess it was a challenge I wasn't up for."

CHAPTER 10
MESSY DIVORCE

I have rarely seen a situation rip apart an entire fan base like the attempted return of Brett Favre did to the Green Bay Packers in the summer of 2008.

Following the blessed 2007 season and Favre's retirement announcement, the Packers put together their offense and entire plan for 2008 around Aaron Rodgers. At the time, head coach Mike McCarthy said, "He's done everything he has had to do in the classroom and practice field; all he has to do now is play!"

Following the loss to the Giants in the NFC title game on the Favre interception, Hall-of-Fame *Journal-Sentinel* beat writer Bob McGinn wrote, "From this point forward, Thompson and McCarthy will have to live with the fact that nothing short of the Super Bowl will be good enough for fans. And having watched Favre look so cold and so old twice in the last month, they probably have doubts how in the world he could ever win another NFC Championship Game in frigid weather."

I can't vouch for what the coaching staff and brain trust believed, but I knew they had a great deal of confidence in Rodgers.

You never know how a player is actually going to pan out until he reaches the field in a starting capacity. But we all had an inclination in Dallas late in 2007 when Rodgers came on for the injured Favre and acquitted himself well. The coaches had also watched Rodgers in practice working over their defense day after day. Rodgers was ready and the last thing he needed was more time on the bench. To most of us looking on, we knew it was time—time for Rodgers.

In terms of the team, everything was "put to bed" by mid-June of 2008. The Packers were set for six weeks of summer vacation before heading back for training camp in July. Everything on the Green Bay front was quiet. Or was it?

On June 20—the final day of offseason practices—Favre called McCarthy and told his coach he still had an "itch" to play and wanted back in.

"When he picked up the phone again after he dropped it, he said, 'Oh, God, Brett. You're putting us in a tight spot,'" Favre later said of his conversation with McCarthy. "He said, 'Brett, playing here is not an option.' Those were his exact, exact words."

McCarthy was about to enjoy some much-needed downtime.

He was going to visit his daughter, Alex, in Texas. McCarthy and his new wife, Jessica, were also set to move into their new home.

But with Favre-a-Palooza beginning, the summer of 2008 was not going to be a vacation for McCarthy.

I started hearing rumors in late June or early July about Favre's desire to return. I had witnessed firsthand how hard it can be for a superstar to leave the game. I saw it with Walter Payton and Michael Jordan in Chicago.

Both Payton and Jordan really struggled with their decisions to retire. Payton was never truly happy after he left football following the 1987 season. He retired on the couched promise that he would get an ownership stake in an NFL franchise. That never happened, and there was a part of Payton that was disappointed not only in that empty promise, but also his decision to retire when he did.

Jordan, meanwhile, retired and unretired three times during his remarkable career. For most athletes, the retirement decision is made for them. They are no longer good enough, so they are released and no one picks them up. Others are forced into retirement by injuries. Only a select few athletes retire with the realization and peace that they have had enough—before someone else tells them they have to leave.

Actually, those are the easy ways out. A great player, the face of the franchise, is almost always left on his own to make that call. I have not met a professional athlete who is truly at ease with stepping away from the game he loves.

Consider this: for the great player and for most players, the thrill of athletic competition, the satisfaction of success, and the roar of the crowd are intoxicating. That adrenaline is something they cannot duplicate in any other walk of life—or the rest of their lives.

The problem for the superstar is that the game becomes who he is. This is an especially difficult problem because players experience an identity crisis when they leave the game. For the superstar, he is the game and the game is him. How can that void be filled after leaving?

Some stay in the game in other capacities—coaching, management, and even ownership. The most recent example of an elite athlete who moved into a front-office position and succeeded is John Elway, the general manager of the World Champion Denver Broncos.

There is no doubt Elway experienced a great deal of joy and satisfaction when the club he built won the 50th Super Bowl. But I can guarantee you that experience could not match the exhilaration he felt when, as a player, he led the Broncos to victory in both Super Bowls XXXII and XXXIII. Nothing can replicate the high the athlete experiences on the field in success. Or the low he feels in failure.

"There is nothing like playing, being in the middle of it," Elway said in a 2014 interview. "That's the truly exciting thing about being in this business, especially playing the quarterback position."

A long career in the NFL might take a great athlete into his mid-to-late 30s. God willing, the athlete has another 40-some years to find a place in life, and that can be both daunting and scary.

I suspected Brett might have trouble in the next phase when in early March 2008 he announced his retirement at a press conference in Green Bay. A reporter asked him, "What are you going to do?"

Brett said, "Nothing. Nothing. [Former general manager] Ron Wolf asked me yesterday, 'What are you going to do?' I said, 'Nothing.' And I'm going to stick to that until I want to do something else."

I don't care who you are or what walk of life you are taking; if on the eve of retirement you have no idea what you will do next, you will struggle.

So part of me was surprised when I first heard Brett wanted to come out of retirement. But in the back of my mind, I knew this was possible. In fact, based on what I had seen in Chicago, it was almost predictable.

Favre was struggling like Payton and Jordan before him. He was exhausted after the 2007 season and depressed after the interception in overtime by Corey Webster in the NFC Championship Game cost the Packers a trip to the Super Bowl.

When Favre announced his retirement, it sure seemed to him like the right time to go.

"I've given everything I possibly can give to this organization, to the game of football, and I don't think I've got anything left to give, and that's it," Favre said at his retirement press conference. "I know I can play, but I don't think I want to. And that's really what it comes down to.

"Fishing for different answers and what-ifs and will he come back and things like that, what matters is it's been a great career for me, and it's over. As hard as that is for me to say, it's over. There's only one way for me to play the game, and that's 100 percent.

"Mike and I had that conversation the other night, and I will wonder if I made the wrong decision. I'm sure on Sundays, I will say I could be doing that, I should be doing that. I'm not going to sit here like other players maybe have said in the past that I won't miss it, because I will. But I just don't think I can give anything else, aside from the three hours on Sundays, and in football you can't do that. It's a total commitment, and up to this point I have been totally committed."

By May, however, the spirit was willing. The body felt good. It was time for Brett Favre to do what he had done at this time of year since high school—get back to work. Only where was he going to work?

I don't blame Favre for wanting to come back. Everyone knew he could still play. But his impending return would put the Packers organization in one heck of a predicament.

Remember, the Packers had put together their entire plan for that season with Rodgers at the helm. Most people on the outside say, "So what's the big deal? Brett's been playing there for years. Just put him back in the lineup." It is not that easy.

For McCarthy, his coaching staff, the team, and especially Rodgers, Favre's return put them in a nearly untenable situation. All of their planning and preparation for the upcoming campaign was complete.

How could McCarthy go back on his young quarterback now—the kid who had waited his turn, had done all the work, and was primed and ready to play? On the other hand, in the eyes of many fans in Green Bay and especially around the country, how could the Packers not welcome back Brett Favre?

Favre vs. Ted Thompson.

Favre vs. Aaron Rodgers.

Favre vs. the Green Bay Packers.

The saga became *the* sports story of 2008. And McCarthy faced challenges that were entirely new to him.

On July 8 of that summer, Favre spoke with McCarthy and Thompson and told them both he wanted back in. Neither man seemed interested.

McCarthy had made significant adjustments to his offense tailored to Rodgers' strengths. McCarthy didn't want to set a precedent in which a player could miss the entire offseason program, then show up for training camp and play—something Favre was now trying to do. And perhaps more than anything, both McCarthy and Thompson wanted to finally see what they had in Rodgers.

Rodgers had been patient. And if Green Bay sent him back to the bench, odds are he would have asked for a chance to play elsewhere.

On July 11, Favre asked the Packers for his release so he could play with another NFL team. The Packers believed Favre wanted to return to the NFC North with either Minnesota or Chicago, and denied his request.

"The finality of his decision to retire was accepted by the organization," the Packers said in a team statement. "At that point, the Green Bay

Packers made the commitment to move forward with our football team."

On July 14, Favre told Fox News that he wanted to play for a team other than the Packers. That led to many Packers fans to hold "Bring Back Brett" rallies outside Lambeau Field.

"I know if I was a fan, on the outside looking in, you don't have all the facts, you're not privy to all the conversations," McCarthy said. "I just hope they respect the fact that we're going about this in a positive manner with the Packers organization's best interests at hand. It's really as simple as that.

"They can disagree. That's okay. I'm not going to sit here and say I've made every decision that's been correct. I'm fine with that. But the disagreeable part of it, when you deal with an organization or a group trying to move forward, that's what holds you back. I respect their passion; I respect everything about our fans. There's nothing like them.

"But my father told me a long time ago that not everybody is going to like you. Get over it. That's life."

Favre also told Fox News that Thompson did not level with him several times, and he didn't feel like he could trust the Packers' general manager.

"Ted and I, I thought, have always had a good relationship," Favre said. "We don't talk a whole lot. We don't go out and eat and shoot the bull. But on three different occasions—I don't want to say lied, I think that's kind of a harsh word, but I think untruth or whatever is better."

As the summer dragged on, the soap opera thickened.

On July 17, the Packers accused the Vikings of tampering, something that was never proven. Favre did not show up for the start of training camp on July 27, but two days later, faxed his official request for reinstatement to the NFL.

As camp opened, McCarthy had chaos on his hands. The national media flooded Green Bay, and the only topic in Wisconsin anyone talked about was Favre.

During McCarthy's season-opening press conference, the first 29 questions were about the Favre saga. In all, McCarthy took 50 Favre-related questions during the press conference.

At one point, an exasperated McCarthy said, "I can anticipate we are going to do this for awhile here."

Then he added: "Aaron Rodgers is the starting quarterback for the Green Bay Packers. That has been stated over and over again. I hope we can finally understand that. That's where we are as an organization. That's where we are as head coach of the Green Bay Packers. I don't know how else to answer your question."

Rodgers also faced an endless stream of questions—and almost none of them were about what was happening on the field.

"I don't need people to feel sorry for me," Rodgers said. "Playing quarterback is a tough job, and there's a lot of scrutiny that goes along with that. You get too much blame a lot of times, you get too much credit a lot of times. And you just have to stay balanced and stay even-keeled.

"The last three years and this offseason have made me the person I am today, and I wouldn't have changed it for anything."

On July 30, Packers president Mark Murphy flew to Mississippi and offered Favre a lucrative marketing deal—10 years and $20 million—to stay retired.

Favre rejected the offer, then flew to Green Bay on July 31.

Two nights later, during the Packers' annual "Family Night" scrimmage at Lambeau Field, Rodgers heard a mixture of boos and cheers when he was introduced.

"Yeah, I take it personally," Rodgers said. "But like I said, it's not the first time and it won't be the last time."

With Favre's shadow looming large, Rodgers struggled that night, missing six straight passes at one point and throwing an interception to safety Aaron Rouse.

One day later, NFL Commissioner Roger Goodell reinstated Favre and Green Bay's quarterback situation was murkier than ever.

"There have been no promises," McCarthy insisted. "Once again, there has been indecision throughout Brett's path back here to Green Bay. It's important for us to sit down, communicate.

"There are some things that we need to go through and then once again, from that information that comes out of that conversation will be used to move forward in the decision we'll make for our football team. That's where we are."

Former Packers longtime public relations official Jeff Blumb couldn't believe all the twists and turns this three-week process took.

"The story took one turn after another," Blumb said. "Whatever you anticipated was going to happen next, the opposite occurred."

It was a conundrum from which there was no easy way out. Stick with your plan that this is now Rodgers' time and his football team? Or bring back arguably the greatest player in the Packers' long and glorious history?

McCarthy's challenges were immense. Not only did he—and the rest of the Packers brass—have to figure out how to best defuse the Favre situation, but McCarthy also had to keep his team focused, on task, and ready for the 2008 campaign.

"It's a challenge any time there's a tension put on your football team that has nothing to do with performance," McCarthy said. "And that's where we need to keep our focus."

Green Bay was coming off a 14-win season and a trip to the NFC Championship Game. But the oodles of media members that descended on Green Bay had little interest in what was happening on the field.

Instead, it was all Favre, all the time. And some players admitted it was hard not to feel slighted.

"It does bother me a little bit because of the quality of football team we have," said center Scott Wells. "We came off an outstanding year last year and we're looking to build on that and we've got a lot of the same players returning.

"Our team's not going to be determined by one player. It's a little frustrating."

Deep down, McCarthy knew keeping his team focused would be virtually impossible if both Favre and Rodgers were on the roster in 2008.

Favre, one of the top players in NFL history, had plenty of good football left in that golden arm. Favre felt that 16 years of high-level play had earned him the right to change his mind on retirement and keep his job.

Rodgers, who was groomed the entire offseason to take the reins, was ready for his opportunity. And if Rodgers didn't get it, Green Bay's quarterback of tomorrow was likely gone.

McCarthy had to figure this out—and do it soon—or risk everything that was built his first 30 months on the job.

At training camp practices, some fans rallied for Favre, holding up signs that read Bring Back Brett. I felt so bad for Rodgers, who had nothing to do with the situation swirling around him.

Team president and CEO Mark Murphy, who had just taken over the organization, said, "I think all of us have said what a difficult situation this has been. We have tried to be fair and we have been very fair to Brett through this process, but ultimately we have always acted in the best interest of the Packers and our organization."

The last thing McCarthy wanted to deal with was a messy transition from the iconic Favre to Rodgers—the player whom he had been grooming to take over under center. But the situation had become ugly and personal and forced one of the most loyal fan bases in sports to pick sides.

So on August 4, 2008, McCarthy and Favre gathered for undoubtedly the most important meeting of McCarthy's Green Bay tenure.

The two began their powwow at 6:00 pm. And it didn't end for six hours.

The two took a break at one point for pizza. Thompson and Favre also talked for about an hour.

McCarthy and Favre even talked again the next morning for about an hour. When it was over, all were in agreement that Favre would keep playing. He just wouldn't do it in Green Bay.

"I thought it was an extremely healthy conversation. I would probably classify it as a conversation that everything you wanted to say, everything you wanted to ask, went on in that conversation," McCarthy said. "I thought it was a conversation that was brutally honest. We agreed to disagree. We stood on opposite sides of the fence on a number of issues, and I respect the way he feels.

"But the one thing that I was looking for out of that conversation was he ready and committed to play football for the Green Bay Packers? And his answer frankly throughout the conversation was his mindset, based on the things that happened throughout this whole course, that's not where he was. So with that, we didn't really move ahead.

"We talked about all of the different options...but the essence of the whole thing was I had a list of questions for him to answer those questions. I had questions that I felt were important for him to answer. I had questions for him from the locker room, from his teammates, and he did a great job. I thought it was a very respectful conversation. The feedback was back and forth. But once again, his feeling was, I don't want to speak for him, but based on where he is, the path that it took to get to this part, he wasn't in the right mindset to play here."

McCarthy and Favre went back and forth on what had transpired since March and how they found themselves in this current position. They covered many of the same issues multiple times.

McCarthy told Favre he could compete for his old spot. And according to McCarthy, Favre had no problem with that.

But it never came to that. At the end of the day, the relationship between Favre and the Packers had been damaged beyond repair.

McCarthy wasn't sure Favre would ever get past what had taken place since March. And deep down, McCarthy must have been terrified of what that could do to his football team.

"I'm not doing the PR thing anymore," McCarthy said. "I'm coaching the football team. The football team has moved forward, okay? The train has left the station, whatever analogy you want. He needs to jump on the train and let's go, or if we can't get past all of the things that have happened, I need to keep the train moving, and he respects that. He understands that.

"When I started the meeting my whole intent was [to find out] was he coming into the locker room to play for the Green Bay Packers, and where is [his] mind at?' That was the first question I asked him, and we could never get back to that point where he was comfortable. It's very personal for him, and understandably so. I have had a very upfront seat throughout this whole process; he has been right in the middle of it. It's emotional for him, very personal. I don't want to be redundant; I don't want to speak for Brett. I respect the way he feels, but he is in a tough spot."

To be honest, both sides were in a brutal spot.

So on August 5, Favre went home to Mississippi as the Packers tried to trade him. And two days later, Favre was sent to the New York Jets for a third-round draft choice.

Thompson also had a comparable offer from Tampa Bay, but undoubtedly wanted Favre out of the NFC.

Thompson was the first to admit he was extremely uncomfortable being known as the guy that traded Favre.

"I don't think anybody would be comfortable with that," Thompson said. "This is, in many ways, sad that this is where it came to. At the end of the day though, I think all parties involved felt like it was the best solution to a very difficult situation."

After weeks of speculation, guesswork, and hypotheticals, Favre was gone. Rodgers was officially the quarterback.

The 2008 season could begin.

"A sense of relief? You could say in a lot of ways," McCarthy said. "I'm about press conferenced out, number one. That's something, it's a responsibility, I understand, but it was something that the situation needed to be resolved and it was nice to get to a finality of that. But I'm relieved that we're talking about football, our football team, and that's what the focus needs to be on."

Following a 9–7 season with the Jets, Favre retired again. He came out of retirement the next summer and signed with Minnesota.

Favre led the Vikings to two wins over the Packers in 2009, and indeed brought Minnesota to the cusp of the Super Bowl. But his interception in the final minute of the NFC title game at New Orleans cost the Vikings—just as an interception in the NFC Championship game cost the Packers two years earlier.

Through the summer of 2008, no one took a higher road than Rodgers. I could not believe how well he handled all of the media after practices. His class and dignity were extremely impressive. Certainly his poise under this kind of pressure and scrutiny would serve him well on the field that season and beyond.

"It was a difficult situation," Rodgers said. "It was tough to stand up every day in front of the media not knowing what questions were coming at me and how the fans were going to react that day in practice. But the whole time the organization stood by me and they told the truth, and I told the truth, and we moved on together.

"I think they knew what kind of person they were getting, and at the same time I hope they knew what kind of player they were getting as well. It gave me a lot of confidence that they stood by me through everything that happened. It was a trying time for myself and the organization, but the fact that they continued to stand by me and believe in me was definitely big for my confidence."

I believe the tumultuous training camp controversy involving Favre doomed the Packers' 2008 season, though. The defense surrendered several late leads in games that season, costing defensive coordinator Bob Sanders his job. But in my opinion, the tumult of August was the greatest factor in the Packers falling from 13–3 in 2007 to 6–10 in 2008.

One of the sayings that comes to mind is, "Time heals all wounds." It took a while. Not so much for the Packers, who went on to win the Super Bowl three seasons later with Rodgers at the controls. But it took a while for Favre himself to come to grips with all that had happened at the end of his storybook career in Green Bay.

Of course, time did eventually work its magic. In the summer of 2015, the Packers inducted Favre into the team's Hall of Fame and retired his No. 4.

All 67,000 tickets to watch Favre's induction on the video boards from inside Lambeau Field were sold in less than two hours. And in one of the most unique nights in team history, Favre became the first-ever Packer to have his number retired and enter the Packers Hall of Fame at the same time.

"All I can say is wow. Wow," Favre told the passionate crowd that night. "This is absolutely amazing. I don't have the words to express the feeling coming out of that tunnel. If there were any doubts before, there's not any. I'm truly thankful."

On Thanksgiving night, in a primetime game against the Bears, they put Favre's name and number up on the north facade of Lambeau Field with the great Bart Starr in attendance.

"I think this is a great tribute to him, to a guy that put a lot of great years into this organization," said Packers fullback John Kuhn, who played with Favre in 2007. "He was so important to the rebirth of the Packers, so I think it's great for him to get his just due, to come back and see his number retired. For that I'm happy for him because he laid a lot of groundwork to chase in here. And that's a good thing."

A painful chapter closed with a celebration befitting his career, contribution, and place in the history of the Green Bay Packers. Brett Favre is a Packer again—as he should be!

But those who witnessed the wild, drama-filled summer of 2008 will never forget it.

CHAPTER 11
AARON RODGERS

I first saw Aaron Rodgers in late September 2003. He was the quarterback for the University of California, and his Golden Bears were playing at Illinois.

I was working play-by-play for ESPN Plus on the Big Ten Game of the Week, and former University of Wisconsin and Green Bay Packers quarterback Randy Wright was the analyst.

Despite record-setting passing numbers at Pleasant Valley High School in his native Chico, California, Rodgers was barely recruited by the major colleges. As a matter of fact, Illinois was the only school that "offered" him, and that was as a walk-on to compete for a possible scholarship in the future.

Rodgers said he was so disappointed back then that he considered quitting football.

"There was a time I thought about that, for sure," Rodgers said. "I had finished my senior year of football, I wasn't playing basketball. It was January and I was working out and stuff and meeting with a couple of coaches.

"The reality was sinking in that, 'Hey, you're not going to get a scholarship.' So now I had some choices to make."

But Rodgers accepted an opportunity to play at nearby Butte College, a two-year community college of approximately 12,000 students in Oroville, California. It was there he grew and blossomed as an athlete.

Butte head coach Craig Rigsbee promised Rodgers he would do everything possible to help him land an NCAA Division I scholarship after one season. So that October, Rigsbee arranged for University of California coach Jeff Tedford to attend practice.

It's been widely reported that Tedford came to see Butte tight end Garrett Cross that day. And while Cross eventually went to Cal, Tedford was there for a different reason.

"He was there to see Aaron," Rigsbee said. "And it was kind of a wild practice.

"We were throwing on every play and running 7-on-7 drills. I mean, we never ran 7-on-7s on Mondays, so guys were wondering what was going on. At the end of practice, Tedford came over to me and said, 'He's the best junior college quarterback I've ever seen.' And I just said, 'Right on!'"

Right on indeed, as Tedford offered Rodgers a scholarship that day.

"Seeing him in person, he was very impressive," Tedford said of Rodgers. "He was very accurate, threw the ball well and had a tight spiral. It was a very pleasant surprise to find out he was very strong in other categories as well."

That's for sure.

The 2003 season was Rodgers' first at Cal and he was competing against an athletic junior quarterback by the name of Reggie Robertson for the starting job. I remember being told that Tedford was alternating the two quarterbacks to see who would emerge. Rodgers was given the starting nod at Illinois, which was the game Wright and I were assigned to that week.

Rodgers led Cal to a 31–24 win that day and completed 20-of-37 passes for 263 yards with one touchdown and no interceptions. His numbers weren't staggering, but my analyst was extremely impressed with Rodgers.

Wright is one of the best analysts I have ever worked with. He's especially good at evaluating quarterbacks in close, tough games. More than numbers, Wright was impressed with the presence that Rodgers had under center.

Illinois had a good defensive unit at the time, and Rodgers' work was outstanding in the eyes of Wright. So I started to keep tabs on this West Coast quarterback throughout the 2003 and '04 seasons.

Rodgers led the Golden Bears to a 7–3 mark in their final 10 games of 2003, throwing for 2,903 yards and 19 touchdowns.

Rodgers, who's extremely protective of the ball, had streaks of 98 and 105 consecutive passes without an interception. He led the Bears to late-season wins against Washington and Stanford to clinch a berth in the Insight Bowl. Then Rodgers threw for 394 yards and was named MVP in Cal's bowl win over Virginia Tech.

Rodgers was even better the following year, when he guided the second-highest-scoring offense in school history. Rodgers threw for 2,566 yards and 24 touchdowns to just eight interceptions, and was named first-team all–Pacific 10.

During that 2004 season, Rodgers authored one of the great performances of the year. In a game at No. 1 USC, Rodgers completed 23 consecutive passes in an eventual 23–17 loss to the Trojans.

Rodgers led Cal to a 10–2 record that season, then gave up his final year of eligibility to enter the NFL draft.

Rodgers headed into the 2005 NFL Draft packed with optimism.

Rodgers was one of the stars of the 2005 NFL Combine. And most "experts" believed Rodgers would be selected at, or near the top of, the first round.

One night during the NFL Combine, Rodgers sat down with members of the Green Bay Packers' front office. But with the Packers slated to pick at No. 24 in two months, both sides figured they wouldn't see each other again.

"I remember telling them, 'Trade up. I'd love to play for you guys,'" Rodgers recalled. "And they were saying, 'Well, you probably won't be available when we want to get you.'"

The Packers weren't looking for a quarterback in the 2005 draft. Brett Favre had just announced that he was coming back for another season and backup Craig Nall was a serviceable No. 2.

The Packers had other needs that year, including a difference-maker on the defensive front. What happened in that draft, though, could only be described as stunning.

The San Francisco 49ers, with head coach Mike Nolan and offensive coordinator Mike McCarthy, selected Utah quarterback Alex Smith with the No. 1 overall pick. Inexplicably, Rodgers then began to slide. And slide. And slide.

Rodgers had gone to New York to be part of the draft festivities. He was also one of a handful of players invited into the green room at the Jacob K. Javits Convention Center, where many of the top players gather.

One by one, the other players in the room were drafted. Eventually, Rodgers was the only one left—and seeing him sit uncomfortably was almost hard to watch.

"Well, obviously when you're sitting in the green room, you just want to get out of there," Rodgers said.

Amazingly, the 22 teams that followed San Francisco also passed on Rodgers.

Green Bay, selecting at No. 24, had Rodgers ranked far higher than that on their draft board. And when Rodgers plummeted, Green Bay's decision makers were almost as shocked as Rodgers himself.

"I got called in a couple picks before our pick into the draft room to ask me once again my opinion and what I thought of him," said Darrell Bevell, who was Green Bay's quarterbacks coach at the time. "I was getting excited from a selfish point of view to get to coach a guy like that and get a guy in the first round and start to groom him. So that was exciting.

"If there was a report that he was going to slip I would have been shocked. I'm still in a little bit of a state of shock that he came down to us."

Shocking for Green Bay and brutal for Rodgers.

Not only was Rodgers scorned by his beloved 49ers at the top of the draft, but he lost millions of dollars by sliding down draft boards. Finally, Green Bay broke Rodgers' fall by taking him at No. 24.

"[Former 49ers safety] Merton Hanks told me, 'You should play your career with a chip on your shoulder regardless and always feel like you've got something to prove,'" Rodgers said the day he was drafted. "And I've got a lot to prove."

After the Packers selected Rodgers, the fans that had assembled for a draft party in the Lambeau Field Atrium began to boo. I was doing a live broadcast in the stadium that day, and I said on the air and to the crowd, "This is a great pick and there will come a day when the Green Bay Packers and all of you will be happy they made this pick."

Rodgers, who had spent a very public, excruciating, and disappointing ordeal that was played out on television, was now a Packer.

While Rodgers was brokenhearted, he was also smart enough to understand there could be some benefits.

Sitting behind the legendary Favre could give Rodgers a chance to develop at his own pace. On the flip side, several young quarterbacks drafted much higher were thrown to the wolves well before they were ready, lost confidence, and were out of the league in no time.

In Green Bay, where Favre was still going strong, Rodgers had no immediate pressures like so many of his peers.

"The more I thought about it, the more I realized it could be a great fit for me, being able to learn from one of the best quarterbacks of all time and to not be thrown in the fire right away and to come to a team with a storied franchise and a winning tradition," Rodgers said. "I think it's going to be exciting. It's going to be a great fit."

The next day, I met Rodgers for the first time and told him my experience of seeing him in that game at Illinois. I said, "It may not seem like it now, but this is a great situation for you."

There was another occurrence, before that draft, that was imperative to the Packers selecting Rodgers. It was a change in the front office.

After a tumultuous 2004 season ending with a dispiriting loss to Minnesota in a home playoff game, Packers president and CEO Bob Harlan relieved Mike Sherman of his duties as general manager. Harlan hired Ted Thompson away from the Seattle Seahawks and Sherman became an embittered outsider in the draft room.

Why was this so important? I guarantee you there is no way Sherman

Aaron Rodgers has won two MVP awards and one Super Bowl title during his first eight years as Green Bay's starting quarterback.

would have picked a quarterback in the first round of that draft.

Sherman the general manager was dominated by the needs of Sherman the coach. The choice of Rodgers was about the future, not the present.

Sherman, as a GM, was not about the future. He was about winning now, before the window closed on Favre.

Sherman probably would have either brokered his draft to trade up and get a defensive lineman, or he would have picked to fill a need. Had Sherman been GM, I believe Rodgers would have slipped beyond the 24th pick in the first round of that draft.

Favre was 35 years old when the Packers drafted Rodgers. He was still playing at a high level, but realized Green Bay had just drafted his likely successor.

Favre was always lauded as a great teammate and leader. In this case, though, Favre wasn't hip on training a player 14 years younger than him to one day take his job.

"Brett and I actually got along well," Rodgers said. "We had a lot better relationship than I think was reported. Obviously, I was drafted to be his successor, and as I get older, you can see how that would be difficult to take if you don't feel like you're ready to move on. I understand that. But [he] and I got along well.

"We had a couple of good conversations over the years. His personality of being a starting quarterback and being a leader, I don't think he felt it was ever his responsibility to get me ready to play. And I never felt like that either. I had a quarterback coach who I could work with. That wasn't Brett's job. His job was to be the best he could be for the No. 1 offense and my job was to support him, get our defense ready to play and give him any tips I could come up with and get myself ready to play just in case something happened."

Rodgers discovered quickly, though, Favre wasn't going to offer up a lot of secrets to his success. So Rodgers tried gleaning every possible nugget by watching and studying everything about Favre's game.

The two men were dramatically different and had largely contrasting styles. But there was still plenty Rodgers pulled from Favre that helped him years down the road.

"I listened a lot," Rodgers said. "I've always felt like whether it was my high school coaches, my junior college coaches, Jeff Tedford and his staff [at Cal]. Whoever you're interacting with, you can take something away, even if you don't mesh with them personality wise or you don't get along with them, you can always take something away from that.

"And I learned a lot about tying footwork to the throws. When you're growing up and watching TV, they'd always talk about how Brett's footwork was crazy. He was throwing from all these platforms and different arm angles. But the genius of it was what he was actually doing is he was always tying his feet to the proper throw and he was throwing off balance so many times that it looked a certain way because no one else was doing it consistently. I think nobody else was working on those types of throws and you could see him doing it in practice.

"We didn't operate in a perfect practice environment, which I think really helps quarterbacking. We're not just dropping back without any pressure in 7-on-7 drills. You're testing yourself, you're extending plays in those drills. You're throwing from awkward angles. You're moving your feet around. You're seeing how your body reacts to hard rolls left and right, move up in the pocket and kind of throw off your wrong foot. And the genius of his footwork is that he practiced those things. So to him, at least, those things really weren't exceptional plays. It's stuff he had ingrained in his muscle memory and that's because of the genius of the footwork he had used.

"Really, that was great. And then the eye control. He had just phenomenal eye control. He would look guys off all the time and throw those passes in practice. I work on all of those things today. You have to work on the awkward body angles that you can get in so that when you're in those in live game situations, you can throw an accurate football."

To this day, Rodgers chuckles when thinking back on that first season in Green Bay.

The Packers had what they called a "Feel Good Saturday." During a light practice before Sunday's game, the scout team offense led by Rodgers was told to throw interceptions to the defense.

The belief was this could get the defense in the right frame of mind for the following day. Rodgers, though, wanted nothing to do with that strategy.

"I knew that those reps on the scout team were going to be invaluable to me in my career, so on the Saturdays, they wanted us to throw interceptions every time and make the defense feel good," Rodgers said. "I kind of rebelled against that because, as you know, I don't like throwing interceptions. Instead, I would throw no-look passes to my guys and work on my eye control and looking one way and throwing another way. And I actually got reprimanded my first year for doing that in a Saturday practice by Mike Sherman.

"But like I always tell the young guys and the new quarterbacks, the only way to develop the habit is to exaggerate it in a practice setting. I always tried to exaggerate those things, and a lot of that I took away from watching Brett."

Sitting and learning from Favre proved to be a terrific thing for Rodgers' career. Another fortuitous occurrence for Rodgers came after Green Bay's brutal 4–12 campaign in 2005.

One day after the season ended, Thompson fired Sherman and hired Mike McCarthy 10 days later. Yes, the same Mike McCarthy who was part of the decision-making group that picked Alex Smith over Rodgers in the previous year's draft.

McCarthy was a notable quarterbacks coach, filling that capacity in 1999 under Ray Rhodes in Green Bay and later with the New Orleans Saints. It was in New Orleans where McCarthy made a starting quarterback out of Aaron Brooks, a former fourth-round pick of the Packers in the 1999 draft.

McCarthy established a quarterback school and Rodgers soaked up the knowledge of his new head coach and quarterbacks coach Tom Clements. The duo taught Rodgers the offense and made a few mechanical adjustments in his delivery, and Rodgers did the rest.

"The thing that really helped was the offseasons," Rodgers said. "In 2006 and '07, as I went through the quarterback school and learned a lot about offense and defense and blitzes and coverages and how to get the most out of my talent…we really started to get on the same page and jell together. It's a great relationship now and there's a lot of love and respect, on and off the field."

For two more seasons, Rodgers "competed" on the scout team each day. His play in practice elevated the preparation of the defensive unit for the upcoming games, because for Rodgers, practice was not about just giving the defense "a look." Practices were his game days!

To Rodgers' credit, his day-to-day consistency was a real strength. Rodgers made the most of his limited repetitions in practice, he continued to master the offense through film study, and he became a popular figure in the Packers' locker room.

"He practices like he's ready," Green Bay tight end Bubba Franks said. "You never know until you put him in, but he's practicing like he's the starter, which has got to give him a little confidence.

"The coach lets him go with the [No.] 1s and he gets good reps. But right now, no one's sure how he'll do until he gets out there and does it."

Rodgers continued to grow, but few on the outside knew how much until late in the 2007 season. Green Bay was 10-1 and went to Dallas for the Cowboys game that would become Rodgers' public debut.

Green Bay fell 37–27, but Rodgers was 18-of-26 for 201 yards, with his first NFL touchdown pass and a passer rating of 104.8.

Later that season, following a disappointing loss to the New York Giants in the NFC Championship Game, the Packers' coaching staff was selected to lead the NFC squad in the Pro Bowl in Hawaii.

Packers offensive coordinator Joe Philbin was observing the quarterbacks for that game at a midweek practice. The NFC quarterbacks were Tony Romo of Dallas, Seattle's Matt Hasselbeck, and Tampa Bay's Jeff Garcia. Over on the AFC side, Peyton Manning of Indianapolis, Pittsburgh's Ben Roethlisberger, and Cleveland's Derek Anderson were the quarterbacks.

Philbin later remarked, "Wow, we have a guy in Green Bay who throws as well as these guys."

That guy was Rodgers. It was at that point that Green Bay's offensive coaching staff knew they had the quarterback of the future on their roster. But little did they know the future was less than a month away.

On March 4, 2008, Favre announced his retirement. That day, an emotional Favre said he had been willing to play another year. But he felt another season would only be successful if he led the Packers to a Super Bowl victory. Favre added that the chances for a Super Bowl win were slim and that he was not up for the challenge.

Years later, on the syndicated program *In Depth with Graham Bensinger*, Favre implied that his hand was forced.

"I should have stood my ground and not retired early," Favre said. "Mike (McCarthy) wants to know and that's—as a head coach of a team or Ted Thompson's job as a GM—I think, rightfully so, they need to know which direction they're going to go in."

I don't believe the Packers tried to force Favre into retirement at all. But I do know they had a young quarterback ready to go. When Favre decided to retire, no one from the Packers' front office was going to travel down to Kiln, Mississippi, to try and talk him out of it.

The Green Bay Packers were now officially Rodgers' team.

"I'm in a good situation, I've got a great team around me," Rodgers said shortly after news of Favre's retirement broke. "A lot of people have been focusing on what I'm going to do. It's what the team is going to do, really. I'm an important part of that and I know my role. I need to play well, and I'm not really going to have a grace period either.

"The expectations that people are going to have are very high. The expectations I have of myself are very high as well. I've definitely been told there haven't been a lot of guys following a legend that play well. Hopefully I'll have like a Steve Young kind of experience here."

By the time Favre changed his mind on retirement in late June, 2008, the Packers had already installed Rodgers as their starting quarterback. McCarthy had spent the entire offseason building his offense around Rodgers.

As we established in Chapter 10, Favre's attempted return was messy, to say the least. It wasn't fair to Rodgers or the Packers. After weeks of consternation, the Packers eventually traded Favre to the New York Jets.

Rodgers had played the role of good soldier through the chaos, saying all the right things and never losing faith that he would keep the starting job the organization handed him months earlier. For that, he won plenty of points.

"I think nationally I earned a lot of respect for that," Rodgers said. "I think I earned a lot of fans nationally, who maybe didn't know me or know a lot about me, by handling things the way I did.

"It was a difficult situation, but I just tried to be as honest and as classy as I possibly could. I realized the situation was way bigger than myself, and I think in doing that, I earned the respect of my teammates, from the organization and from our fans. And I think people that didn't know me nationally took notice, too."

Being named the starting quarterback is one thing. Becoming the starting quarterback is quite another. By *becoming,* I mean your teammates buying in. That has to be proven on the field often under adverse situations.

Rodgers and the Packers were 2–2 to start the 2008 season. In Tampa Bay in Week 4, Rodgers suffered a sprained right shoulder in the third quarter on a seven-yard scramble. Rodgers left the game, then came back for one more series, but could not complete the 30–21 loss to the Buccaneers.

The following week, Atlanta came to Green Bay. Rodgers was limited all week in practice. His status was highly questionable right up to the morning of the game.

I remember Rodgers went to the Don Hutson Center across the street from Lambeau Field with team doctors and quarterback coach Tom Clements for a private workout to determine if he could physically play.

The media buildup to the game focused on Rodgers' durability compared with the ultimate quarterback ironman, Brett Favre. The question being asked was: Is Aaron going to miss more games in his first season as the starter than Favre missed in 16 years under center for the Packers?

Rodgers went over to the Hutson Center that morning determined to convince the medical people that he could play.

There's no question that Rodgers' teammates were watching closely, as well. Rodgers not only played that day, but he played well. He persevered through the pain and went 25-of-37 for 313 yards and three touchdowns.

Green Bay lost the game 27–24 when its defense collapsed late in the fourth quarter. But Rodgers' teammates knew they had a quarterback.

"He played big in that game," McCarthy said of Rodgers. "Being down at the workout on Sunday, I just left an open mind to it. I didn't feel very good about where he was on Friday, but all along you collect the information that you're given from the player, from the doctor, from the rehab specialists and the trainers and so forth, and he was in a lot of pain. For him to go out and throw the ball the way he did and play the way he did is a tribute to him, and he definitely played big in the game. Very impressed with it."

On that day, Aaron Rodgers proved to the locker room that he could lead this team. Since then, there has never been a question inside the team about leadership at quarterback under Rodgers.

I have been around a lot of sports stars in my career and few value relationships like Rodgers does. When a new player comes into the Packers' locker room—even a street free agent—Rodgers makes sure he knows something about the guy.

Rodgers is one of the first players in the locker room to introduce himself and try to make the new player feel at home. That's a quiet form of leadership that we on the outside don't always get to see. I think it speaks to the character of the man.

Make no mistake; Rodgers has an inner drive that is similar to what I observed in Walter Payton and Michael Jordan. Like all of the greats, there is a near desperation to compete, and most of all, to win!

We saw that drive firsthand during Green Bay's postseason run following the 2010 season—specifically in the NFC Divisional playoff game at top-seeded Atlanta.

Green Bay went to Atlanta for the divisional playoffs as a two-point underdog. But Rodgers and the Packers blew the lid off the Georgia Dome.

Rodgers, making just his third postseason start, had a game for the ages. Rodgers completed 31-of-36 passes for 366 yards, threw three touchdowns and no interceptions, and posted a passer rating of 136.8 in Green Bay's stunning 48–21 win.

Rodgers set Packers playoff records for completions (31) and completion percentage (86.1 percent), and had the second-most passing yardage in team history (366). In 10 possessions, Rodgers led Green Bay to five offensive touchdowns and two field goals, and the Packers never punted.

"This probably was my best performance—the stage we were on, the importance of this game," Rodgers said afterward. "It was a good night."

That's putting it mildly.

"You look at that Atlanta game, which everybody has, and I think that's the best I've seen a quarterback play," Packers left tackle Chad Clifton said. "Just the plays he made with his arm and with his legs, he's a special player."

Rodgers wasn't nearly as sharp the following week, when the Packers defeated Chicago 21–14 in the NFC Championship Game. Rodgers had just a 55.4 passer rating, but he did have an early rushing touchdown, helped the Packers race to a 14–0 lead, and eventually held on for his biggest win ever.

"I can play a lot better than I did [against Chicago], that's for sure," Rodgers said. "You've got to give credit to Chicago's defense. They had a good plan for us, but I didn't throw the ball as well as I wanted to."

Perhaps Rodgers' most memorable moment in that game came on a play he doesn't have to make all that often.

Green Bay led 14–0 at halftime. On the Packers' first series of the second half, Rodgers drove Green Bay inside Chicago's 10-yard line and was looking for a decisive score.

Bears All-Pro linebacker Brian Urlacher intercepted a Rodgers aerial and was on his way to the end zone with just one man to beat. That man was Rodgers.

In what might have been the play of the game, Rodgers dove at Urlacher's ankles and tripped him up at the Chicago 45-yard line. The Packers defense forced the Bears to punt on the ensuing possession. It was a play that could have turned the momentum of the game in Chicago's favor. It was a play the Packers needed on their way to Super Bowl XLV.

"I don't get paid to tackle, but that was probably one of my better plays of the game," Rodgers said.

Two weeks later, Rodgers was nearly flawless leading the Packers to their 13th NFL title. Rodgers was a picture of precision against a Pittsburgh Steelers defense that was the NFL's best in 2010.

In a game of inches, Steelers defenders were often just inches away from breaking up one Rodgers pass after another. Instead, Rodgers completed 24-of-39 passes for 304 yards and threw three touchdowns and no interceptions. In a word, he was brilliant, and he was named the game's MVP after leading Green Bay to a 31–25 win.

"He played great," McCarthy said. "We put everything on his shoulders. He did a lot at the line of scrimmage for us against a great defense. He did a hell of a job."

Rodgers' passer rating of 111.5 was the fourth-highest in Super Bowl history. His 304 passing yards might have been 450 if it weren't for a bevy of drops.

"He made plays," Steelers head coach Mike Tomlin said of Rodgers. "We didn't get turnovers. We know that they're capable of getting plays in chunks. We knew that they would throw the football quite a bit and they did. He didn't fold under the pressure.

"I thought we hit him some early, we got to him as the game went on. But he showed his [mettle] and continued to stand in there and throw the football and throw it accurately. I tip my hat to him for that."

Amazingly, Rodgers was even better the following season.

The Packers finished the 2011 regular season 15–1—the best mark in franchise history. And Rodgers had arguably the finest season in team history.

Rodgers led the NFL in quarterback passer rating (122.5), finished No. 2 in touchdowns (45), and led in yards per attempt (9.25). He also finished No. 2 in completion percentage (68.3) and No. 5 in passing yards (4,643).

Rodgers' 45 passing touchdowns set a single-season franchise record and ranked No. 4 in NFL history at the time. His passing yardage total also ranked No. 1 in team history, and he threw just six interceptions. In addition, Rodgers had just three games when his quarterback rating was below 100.0.

"Every Monday, when you watched the game from Sunday, you'd see the things that he did and how accurate he was and how productive he was," said Tom Clements, who was Green Bay's quarterbacks coach in 2011. "Just all along you knew he was having a great year.

"Obviously when you kind of live vicariously through your players, you're happy for them. When someone does well, you're happy for them and it kind of makes you feel great."

Rodgers became just the third Packer to ever win NFL MVP honors. Bart Starr won the award in 1966, while Favre captured three straight MVPs between 1995–97.

"He's playing as well as anyone ever has," said Edgar Bennett, who played five seasons with Favre and was Green Bay's wide receivers coach in 2011. "All I know is we are extremely blessed and fortunate to have a guy like Aaron Rodgers as our quarterback. This guy is phenomenal. He really is."

Wideout James Jones, who also played with Favre, agreed with Bennett.

"There ain't nobody better right now," Jones said. "I'm not sure if there's ever been anybody better here.

"I'm not saying he's better than Brett, but Aaron's my quarterback and I'm always going to have his back. And I'm saying I'd take him over anybody because I got his back like that. He's my quarterback and I'll take him over anybody that's playing today, yesterday, or in the future."

As good as Rodgers and the Packers' record-setting offense was in 2011, the divisional playoff game against the New York Giants at Lambeau Field was another story. Rodgers completed 26-of-46 passes that day for 264 yards with two touchdowns and an interception. His 78.5 passer rating, though, was his lowest of the season.

In addition to the interception, for the first and only time all season, Rodgers lost a fumble. He was unable to elevate his team to victory. And the Green Bay offense, which had turned the ball over only 14 times all year, lost four turnovers that day.

The winningest regular season in Green Bay history came to a sudden, unexpected end in a 37–20 loss to the eventual Super Bowl champion Giants.

"We got beat by a team that played better tonight," Rodgers said afterward. "That's the reality of this league. Been in it for a while and been in the playoffs four times, and three times you lose your last game and you go home, and the one time you have that euphoric feeling that you keep fighting for.

"It's tough. Didn't think it was going to end tonight, felt good about our chances, felt good about our team. Personally, I didn't play as well as I wanted to."

Rodgers had been so good for the past year-and-a-half that Packer Nation now expected greatness on a weekly basis. On this night, though, Green Bay's faithful witnessed the type of quarterbacking that much of the league lives with each week.

The Giants played mostly man coverage with two deep safeties. And when Rodgers refused to take chances, New York's pass rushers sacked him four times.

"Did we rattle him? Maybe a little bit," said Giants cornerback Aaron Ross, whose team had lost to the Packers 38–35 one month earlier. "I just think we did a good job locking on to the receivers and taking away some places he wanted to go."

Over the next four seasons, Rodgers continued to play at an extremely high level.

In 2012, Rodgers and the Packers captured the NFC North with an 11–5 record, one game better than runners-up Minnesota and Chicago. And Rodgers produced another huge season.

Rodgers threw for 39 touchdowns and just eight interceptions in 2012. Rodgers led the NFL in passer rating (108.0) for a second straight year, becoming the first quarterback to accomplish that since Peyton Manning, who did it from 2004 to '06.

Rodgers finished third in the NFL in completion percentage (67.2), the second-best total in team history behind only his 2011 mark. Rodgers also threw for 4,295 yards and led the NFL in touchdown percentage (7.1).

Once again, though, the Packers stumbled in the NFC Divisional Round. San Francisco quarterback Colin Kaepernick accounted for 444 total yards—including 181 on the ground—and the 49ers cruised to a 45–31 win. Kaepernick also threw for two touchdowns and ran for two more.

"We just didn't get it done in the second half," Rodgers said. "I knew we were going to have to score some points. We knew we were going to have to put up at least 38 points."

The 2013 season was a frustrating one for Green Bay.

The Packers were rolling along, had won four straight games, and were sitting at 5–2 in early November. But on Green Bay's first series during a Monday-night game against Chicago, Rodgers was sacked by Bears defensive lineman Shea McClellin and broke his collarbone.

Rodgers returned for the regular season finale and led the Packers to a win in Chicago that helped them sneak into the playoffs.

Green Bay trailed Chicago 28–27 with 46 seconds left in a showdown for the NFC North title—and the division's only playoff berth. The Packers faced fourth-and-8 from Chicago's 48-yard line, which in essence meant it was a win-or-go-home play.

The Bears rushed seven and the Packers blocked with just six. Rodgers was nearly leveled by Bears right end Julius Peppers, but escaped to his left.

Downfield, Bears safety Chris Conte let wideout Randall Cobb slip behind him. And when Rodgers delivered a strike to Cobb, the shifty receiver raced home for a remarkable 48-yard touchdown that gave the Packers a stunning 33–28 win.

It was arguably Green Bay's biggest play in the closing moments of a must-win game since Brett Favre hit Sterling Sharpe for a 40-yard touchdown in the 1993 wild card playoffs.

"Aaron and Randall just made a phenomenal play," Mike McCarthy said. "Those two guys making a great, great play that will be running on the highlight reel for the rest of my time on this earth. What a great finish."

The play gave Green Bay (8–7–1) a third straight NFC North championship and its seventh divisional title since 2002. It also vaulted the

Packers into the postseason, where they earned the No. 4 seed to fifth-seeded San Francisco in a wild card game.

"I was able to get the edge and saw Randall running wide open," Rodgers said. "I knew I had to get a little bit on it just to make sure that I didn't way under-throw him. When that ball came down in the end zone, it was just pandemonium."

The final play capped a memorable 15-play, 87-yard drive that took nearly six minutes. Along the way, the Packers converted three fourth down plays.

First, fullback John Kuhn gained one yard on fourth-and-1 from Green Bay's own 22-yard line. Later, Rodgers hit wideout Jordy Nelson for six yards on another fourth-and-1.

Then of course came the heroics of Rodgers and Cobb, who combined for the biggest play of the Packers' roller coaster season.

"To pick up three fourth downs on that last drive. Wow," Packers nose tackle Ryan Pickett said. "What are the odds of that?"

But San Francisco, the defending NFC champs, knocked Green Bay out of the playoffs for a second straight year. Once again, the Packers struggled to contain Kaepernick and the visiting 49ers edged Green Bay 23–20.

"Yeah, I mean it's frustrating," Rodgers said afterward. "I think you have to start with yourself and...I could have definitely made a few more plays. So that's why it's disappointing.

"These opportunities are pretty special and you've got to make the most of them. It's nine years for me now, blessed to play that long, and would love to play another time if possible. But this is an opportunity we let slip through our fingers."

In 2014, Rodgers had arguably the best season of his career and won his second MVP Award in four years. Rodgers completed 341-of-520 passes (65.6 percent) for 4,381 yards and 38 touchdowns. He also threw just five interceptions and finished with a 112.2 passer rating.

Rodgers again ranked No. 1 in touchdown-to-interception ratio (7.60, 38-to-5) and finished second in the NFL in passer rating and yards per attempt (8.43). Rodgers was third in touchdown passes and was the only quarterback in the NFL to finish in the top three in all four of those categories.

"I need to figure out new ways to compliment Aaron, frankly," McCarthy said.

In the NFC Championship Game, though, the Packers snatched defeat from the jaws of victory and lost to Seattle 28–22 in overtime.

Green Bay held a 16–0 halftime lead. And according to ProFootball Reference.com, the Packers' chances of winning at that point were 94.4 percent.

Green Bay also led 19–7 with just more than three minutes left in the game. And at that moment, the Packers' chances of winning were 99.9 percent.

But somehow, someway, the Seahawks rallied for the most improbable of wins.

In overtime, Seahawks wideout Jermaine Kearse beat Packers cornerback Tramon Williams for a 35-yard, game-winning touchdown after the Packers blitzed and had no safety help.

"I tried to watch the film…but I didn't," Packers left guard Josh Sitton said. "I couldn't watch it. I knew what happened. We kicked their ass up front, and the whole game. We handled them all day. We should've won the game."

Rodgers agreed.

"It's a missed opportunity that I will probably think about the rest of my career," Rodgers said. "We were the better team…and we played well enough to win and we can't blame anybody but ourselves."

Packers No. 1 wideout Jordy Nelson suffered a torn ACL during the 2015 preseason. Rodgers and the Packers' offense were never quite the same.

Rodgers finished with a 92.7 quarterback rating, 13.3 points below his career average entering the 2015 season. Rodgers' 3,821 passing yards were his fewest in a season where he started at least 15 games.

Rodgers' completion percentage of 60.7 was his lowest since becoming a starter. And his average yards per passing attempt (6.7) was 18.3 percent less than his average from 2005 to '14 (8.2).

Green Bay settled for second place in the NFC North at 10–6, one game behind Minnesota. The Packers then defeated Washington in the wild-card round of the playoffs before falling in overtime to Arizona in the divisional playoffs.

"I tell you this is the most adversity he had to play through probably since '08," McCarthy. "In the picture of things…I thought he did a heck of a job dealing with that.

"Aaron, he's that great player [who] plays at such a high level the competition is usually with himself trying not to do too much. And I think he was really challenged this year more than ever with what he was trying to pick up for with Jordy and so forth."

Rodgers is a virtuous human being. He is very smart and extremely loyal to those who have supported or befriended him along the way. This is the person I have observed since he arrived in Green Bay in 2005.

I offered words of encouragement when he arrived following that disappointing draft experience. While he toiled in obscurity as Favre's backup, we kept up a cordial, friendly relationship. I, for one, appreciated that.

When he became a superstar after Super Bowl XLV, nothing in our relationship changed. We still talk just about every week during the season for a few minutes. He gives me his thoughts on his team and that week's opponent. His comments help shape my preparation for the Packers Radio Network broadcast. He doesn't have to grant me that time, but he does—and I certainly appreciate it.

There are two moments with Rodgers that I will always remember fondly. I took my son, Bryan, down to the locker room in Chicago to shake hands with and congratulate Rodgers after the 2010 NFC Championship Game. Rodgers was gracious to the both of us.

Two weeks later, when I saw him in the victorious Super Bowl locker room, I said, "I told you this was going to happen." He said, "I know."

Here's a guy I first met at the lowest point of his professional career following the disappointing 2005 draft. We maintained a cordial relationship over the years, and now we exchanged greetings at the ultimate moment in his professional life. The shared experience made those moments just a little more special.

One last point on Rodgers—people ask me all the time to compare him to Brett Favre or other quarterbacks in the league. To me, Aaron Rodgers is the modern day version of one of my boyhood heroes—Bart Starr. That is the highest compliment I can give a Green Bay quarterback!

I would be surprised if Rodgers and the Packers don't have several Super Bowls in their future—hopefully beginning soon.

CHAPTER 12
2010: SUPER SEASON

Failure Before Success

In my career, I have covered two teams that went on to win the Super Bowl—the legendary 1985 Chicago Bears and the 2010 Green Bay Packers. Each of those teams experienced bitter defeats prior to attaining ultimate success. Without question, the seeds of those "super" teams were sown long before the actual seasons in which they made their run.

In the case of the Bears, future Hall of Fame general manager Jim Finks, along with his director of college scouting, Bill Tobin, began putting the pieces of the Bears' championship team together as far back as 1979. That year, they selected Dan Hampton, a defensive lineman out of Arkansas, in the first round of the draft.

Linebacker Otis Wilson and fullback Matt Suhey came in the next draft. Offensive tackle Keith Van Horne, middle linebacker Mike Singletary, and safety Todd Bell were drafted in 1981.

Quarterback Jim McMahon was selected in 1982, while offensive tackle Jimbo Covert and wide receiver Willie Gault were first-round picks in 1983. Also in that incredible draft, cornerback Mike Richardson, safety Dave Duerson, and guard Tom Thayer were picked.

In the eighth round that year, Mark Bortz, a defensive lineman out of Iowa who would go on to a stellar career at offensive guard for the Bears, and a little-known defensive end by the name of Richard Dent came on board. Dent would go on to become a dominant force and Super Bowl XX MVP.

The team was completed with the selection of linebackers Wilbur Marshall and Ron Rivera in the first two rounds of the 1984 draft, and defensive tackle William Perry came into the fold in 1985. Of those players, Hampton, Dent, and Singletary are in the Pro Football Hall of Fame. Most of those players went to multiple Pro Bowls, and all of them were starters at one point or another in their Chicago careers.

The 1985 Bears were the most talented team I have ever been around—in any sport. Their ascent to the championship had its roots in the draft, but also in a crushing loss in the 1984 NFC Championship game at San Francisco. There, the eventual Super Bowl champion 49ers schooled Chicago 23–0.

This young group of Bears was a collection of incredible personalities and egos, a locker room full of alpha males. That loss at San Francisco in the championship game galvanized them, focused them on one game, a goal they believed was their destiny—Super Bowl XX.

Chicago's dominant march through a 15–1 season was breathtaking, and its 46–10 win over New England in the 20th Super Bowl was the largest margin in Super Bowl history to that point. For the Bears, it was mission accomplished, but that fact only released what bound them together and they were never the same. As good as the 1985 Bears were, they never got back to the Super Bowl.

The 2010 Green Bay Packers' story actually began back in 2005, when team president and CEO Bob Harlan hired Ted Thompson as his general manager. Thompson was one of Ron Wolf's top aids in building the Super Bowl XXXI and XXXII Packers teams.

Thompson left for Seattle to oversee the Seahawks draft from 2000 to '04. During that time, Thompson was instrumental in building a team that won four straight division titles and reached Super Bowl XL following the 2005 season.

Thompson's first draft pick in Seattle was running back Shaun Alexander, who led the league in rushing and was the league MVP in 2005. When Thompson left Seattle to return to Green Bay, Seahawks coach Mike Holmgren said, "There is no question Ted Thompson will build a Super Bowl roster in Green Bay."

With the Packers, Thompson established a draft-and-develop program. His first draft choice was quarterback Aaron Rodgers, who fell to him on the 24th pick in the first round of the 2005 draft. Safety Nick Collins came in the second round of that draft, while linebacker A.J. Hawk, left guard Daryn Colledge, and wide receiver Greg Jennings were added in the 2006 draft.

Kicker Mason Crosby, now the club's all-time leading scorer, was drafted in 2007, while wide receiver Jordy Nelson, tight end Jermichael Finley, and guard Josh Sitton were taken in 2008. Nose tackle B.J. Raji and linebacker Clay Matthews were both first-round draft picks in 2009—Matthews the result of a rare trade back into the first round—while offensive tackle Bryan Bulaga, defensive end/outside linebacker Mike Neal, and safety Morgan Burnett were taken in 2010 and put the finishing touches on what would become a Super Bowl roster.

While Thompson takes a lot of criticism for not venturing into free agency very often, the fact is he added a couple of key free agents who made a huge difference in that Super Bowl XLV championship squad. Charles Woodson, the All-Pro cornerback from the Oakland Raiders, and defensive lineman Ryan Pickett from the St. Louis Rams were both enormous reasons the 2010 Packers became Super Bowl champions.

On the field, Woodson was the NFL Defensive Player of the Year in 2009, while Pickett was a staple of the Packers' defensive line. Off the field, both were terrific behind-the-scenes leaders with a very young group around them.

Woodson and Pickett were consummate professionals. Woodson took Collins and cornerback Tramon Williams under his wing and taught them how to prepare, study, and play the game at the professional level. By 2010 they joined Woodson on the NFC Pro Bowl team. Pickett became the leader of a defensive line that played at an extremely high level throughout 2010.

Growing Pains

In the 2009 preseason, Green Bay's offense was rolling, scoring 31 and 44 points in consecutive wins over Buffalo and at Arizona. There was some real hype around the league about Green Bay. But the Packers started just 2–2 in the first month of the regular season.

The first half of the season included two bitter losses to Brett Favre and the Minnesota Vikings. Perhaps still disheartened by a second loss to the Vikings in Green Bay on November 1, the Packers traveled to winless Tampa Bay the following week and suffered a humiliating 38–28 loss to the Buccaneers.

That loss in Tampa had everyone questioning where these Packers were going. And at 4–4, the Super Bowl hype from August was a thing of the past.

As the .500 Packers prepared to host Dallas, the fan base was in a tizzy. Before the game, fans paraded outside Lambeau Field wearing "Fire McCarthy" and "Fire Thompson" buttons.

And with Favre and the Vikings running away with the NFC North, Packer Nation wasn't exactly thrilled to have Rodgers running the show.

"I can tell you that '09 was a tense season for everybody, especially coming off of '08 the way we played," said Rodgers, whose team was 6–10 in 2008. "That was a pretty tense year. We all kind of felt like we were playing for our jobs."

In particular, it was a "come to Jesus" moment for the defense. New coordinator Dom Capers was implementing a base 3–4, and needed his players to start believing in the new system, even as a once-promising campaign was spiraling downward.

The Cowboys came to Lambeau Field winners of four straight games and leading the NFC East with a 6–2 mark. The Packers entered as a 3-point underdog on their own field, knowing another loss might keep them from the postseason.

Rodgers keyed a pair of huge fourth-quarter touchdown drives, running for one score and throwing for another. Green Bay held Dallas to season lows in rushing yards (61) and total yards (278).

And the Packers exited with a critical 17–7 victory.

"I don't necessarily point to that game, but I know we got on a run there which got us going really good," Rodgers said. "And that was an important win for us. Our defense hit a stretch there where we started playing really good."

Green Bay's defense was especially impressive that day. Woodson had a huge interception, and the Packers sacked Dallas quarterback Tony Romo five times and held the Cowboys to just 278 yards of offense. The victory turned Green Bay's season around, and the Packers' defense took off in the second half of the season.

Capers' unit went on to lead the league in rushing yards allowed (83.3). They were second in overall yardage (284.4) and seventh in points allowed (18.6). It was the best defensive performance by Green Bay since the Super Bowl XXXI champions.

For Woodson, a likely future Hall of Fame Player, it might have been his finest hour with nine interceptions, first-team All-Pro honors and his Player of the Year award.

"Tell me another corner that can go out and cover somebody's best receiver inside or outside, that can go in and take a tight end away, that can blitz and tackle the way he does," Packers defensive backs coach Joe Whitt Jr. said. "Not many people can go in there and learn five different positions and come out of a game with no [missed assignments], and that's what he does."

Woodson, Collins, and Matthews all made the Pro Bowl and Capers was selected Sporting News Coordinator of the Year. The Packers won seven of their last eight games that season and qualified for the playoffs with an 11–5 record.

Postseason Setback

Similar to what the 1985 Bears experienced, the Packers suffered a bitter postseason loss preceding their run to the mountaintop.

Green Bay took on defending NFC champion Arizona in Glendale,

Arizona, in a wild-card playoff game that lived up to its namesake. It was wild!

Rodgers set a Packers postseason record with 423 passing yards, throwing four touchdowns and running for one. But Cardinals old pro Kurt Warner, who would retire at the end of the season, destroyed Green Bay's overmatched secondary and completed a remarkable 29-of-33 passes (87.9 percent) for 379 yards, five touchdowns, and no interceptions.

Unfortunately for Rodgers and the Packers, the game ended when Rodgers was stripped of the football by Arizona's Michael Adams. Karlos Dansby recovered the fumble and went 17 yards for a touchdown that gave the Cardinals a victory in the highest-scoring postseason game in NFL history.

"This is just going to make myself and these guys want it that much more," Rodgers said of the loss to Arizona. "It might not look like we came that close, but we still feel like we were close to achieving all the goals we set forth at the beginning of the season."

For a young team with a great deal of confidence, it was a sudden end to their season. But I do not think the Packers make their "super" run the following year if not for the trials of 2009.

That team grew up, learned how to win, and fully understood the agony of defeat.

Sights Set

Prior to the outset of the 2010 season, McCarthy put framed team pictures of the Packers' 12 World Championship teams on the walls of the team meeting room. This is the room where the whole team meets each day before breaking into individual classrooms for the different units of offense, defense, and special teams.

McCarthy put a 13th frame on the wall and left it blank, telling his

155

team, "That's where our picture goes this year." The meaning was obvious to all in attendance. This was the first of many behind-the-scenes moves McCarthy made to motivate his team during that 2010 season.

The Super Bowl was slated for AT&T Stadium in Dallas, and so confident were the young Packers that they dressed up in cowboy boots and hats for their Welcome Back luncheon in Green Bay prior to their season opener at Philadelphia. It was a public display of the "Super Bowl or bust" mentality that drove this team.

The Regular Season

The Packers had not won a game in Philadelphia in almost 50 years. The last Green Bay team to win in Philadelphia was Vince Lombardi's 1962 Packers team that blanked the Eagles 49–0 at Franklin Field.

In the 2010 opener, the Packers built a 20–3 lead only to see Eagles quarterback Kevin Kolb leave the game due to a jaw injury on a tackle by Clay Matthews in the second quarter.

That brought on longtime thorn in the Packers' side Michael Vick. The same Michael Vick who, while with Atlanta earlier in his career, authored the first postseason victory by a visiting NFL team on Wisconsin soil. Vick led the Falcons to a 27–7 win over one of Mike Sherman's 12–4 Packers teams at Lambeau Field in January 2003.

Vick was at it again, throwing for 175 yards and a touchdown while rushing for 103 yards. But this time the Packers hung on for a 27–20 win.

Pretty or not, the 2010 season was off to a successful start.

"I thought it was a very gutty performance on both sides of the field and we feel very fortunate to come out of here with a win," McCarthy said. "This is a tough place to play and it's a tough football team to play against."

Green Bay didn't leave unscathed, though. Standout running back Ryan Grant was lost for the year with an ankle injury, and the Packers would have to move forward without their No. 1 running back.

"Ryan Grant is exactly the type of individual you want on your team and in your program, the way he goes about his business," McCarthy said. "He is a hard-working, tough guy, no-nonsense, no-excuse individual, and he is a very good teammate. So the personal angle of Ryan's injury is definitely difficult."

Following a 34–7 rout of Buffalo in the home opener, the Packers dropped a 20–17 decision to the Bears in Chicago on a Monday night.

The Packers set a new team record with 18 penalties. Chicago's Devin Hester returned a punt 62 yards for a touchdown, his first return for a score in three years. And Packers wideout James Jones had a critical late-game fumble that set up Chicago's Robbie Gould for a chip-shot field goal that gave the Bears a three-point win.

"It was an uncharacteristic game on offense for us, well, just as a team," Rodgers said. "Way too many penalties."

Green Bay returned home and notched a hard-fought 28–26 win over Detroit. But the Packers suffered back-to-back overtime losses—first at Washington and then home against Miami.

This group with "super" expectations was suddenly on the ropes at 3–3.

Furthermore, the Packers were starting to resemble a MASH unit.

The Packers lost veteran right tackle Mark Tauscher (shoulder), inside linebacker Nick Barnett (wrist), and rookie safety Morgan Burnett (ACL) in Week 4, and all three didn't play again in 2010.

In Week 5, Rodgers suffered a concussion in the loss, while Finley (knee), defensive end Mike Neal (shoulder), and special teams ace Derrick Martin (knee) suffered season-ending injuries.

The Packers finished the regular season with 15 players on the injured reserve list. Eight of those injured players started at least one game that season and six of them were full-time starters.

"We've just got to pull through and find a way to win," running back Brandon Jackson said. "I don't know how. We've just got to win. Just got to win. All I know is we have to play better. We have to run better, we have throw better, we have to catch better.

"We're way better than what the record says, but we are what the record says. We've just got to come out and play better for four quarters and not give an opponent a chance to come back and win the ball game."

Moment of Truth

It was Week 7 and the real moment of truth was upon this Packers team. Brett Favre and the defending NFC North Division champion Minnesota Vikings were coming to Green Bay.

I felt that Green Bay—and certainly Packers Nation—needed this game for closure. After all that had happened with Favre's bitter departure in 2008 and the two losses to the Vikings in 2009, this was much bigger than an average regular season game.

The only way to get over this Favre thing was to beat Brett and the Vikings—at least in Lambeau Field.

It was a Sunday-night game that went back-and-forth throughout. Rodgers, playing with the weight of the world on his shoulders, for obvious reasons, threw two first-half interceptions and the Vikings led 17–14 at intermission.

Midway through the third quarter, Rodgers found Greg Jennings on a 14-yard touchdown pass. Later, linebacker Desmond Bishop intercepted Favre and returned the pass 32 yards for a touchdown, giving the Packers a 28–17 lead.

But Favre was not going to go quietly into the night. The former Green Bay legend hit Randy Moss on a four-yard touchdown pass to cut the deficit to 28–24.

In a tense, scoreless fourth quarter, Favre was doing what he did so often for the Packers—driving his team to a game-winning score in the final minutes. He threw an apparent touchdown pass to Percy Harvin with 48 seconds remaining for what would have been the winning score. But the officials reviewed the play and reversed the call on the field. It was the third time in that game they had taken Vikings points off the board on a review.

On fourth-and-15 at the Green Bay 20, Favre threw incomplete trying to hit Randy Moss at the back line of the north end zone and the Packers won 28–24.

"A loss could have been devastating," said Packers cornerback Tramon Williams, who was in coverage on Moss on the Vikings' final offensive play. "It would have been another loss to Minnesota. Whew."

What struck me about that game was Favre. There he was at 41 years old, on a bad ankle, firing away with a team that was going nowhere that season, and in fact, with the loss fell to 2–4. Favre left Lambeau Field for the final time guns blazing, just as you would expect he would. It was a sight to behold!

"There were some plays where it was like, 'Oh man, come on. Somebody make a play,'" Packers safety Nick Collins said of the final minutes. "At the end of the day, we rose up to the occasion. That was a plus.

"The win, the last couple plays, everything was big tonight because we talk about what we want to do as a team. So tonight was a step in the right direction."

On a Roll

Over the next three weeks, the Packers seemed to find their chemistry. Banged up and battered coming off the emotional Minnesota game, the Packers went to the Meadowlands on a windy day. And while the offense sputtered, the defense was magnificent in a 9–0 shutout of the New York Jets.

I'll never forget Howard Green, an enormous defensive lineman cut by the Jets the previous week. He was in his car driving home to Mississippi when he took a phone call from the Packers that Wednesday offering him a chance to play. Green turned his car around, arrived in Green Bay on Friday, got onto the Packers' plane to the Meadowlands on Saturday, and made four tackles in the game against his former team the next day.

The Jets had entered the game a six-point favorite, but Green Bay forced three turnovers and blanked Rex Ryan's bombastic bunch. New York, widely considered the AFC's top team, had been humbled on its home field, and the Packers were once again riding high.

"We love to be underdogs," Collins said. "Everybody thinks the Jets are the team to win the Super Bowl. We wanted to come in here and match their intensity and show them that we can play with anybody."

Still, I wondered how a team so beat up that they had to pick up players off the street and immediately plug them into their lineup was ever going to realistically contend for the Super Bowl.

As for Green? He would make a much bigger impact later that season in a much bigger game.

The next week, the Packers were back home for another nationally televised Sunday-night game—this one against Dallas—and it was no contest.

With 2:04 remaining in the first half, the Packers took a 28–0 lead as Collins picked up a fumble and returned it 26 yards to score the earliest "dagger" I have ever called.

The Packers rolled up 415 yards of total offense, their second-highest total of the season. Green Bay had a season-high 26 first downs and converted a season-best 66.7 percent of its third downs (10-of-15).

Rodgers threw for 289 yards and three touchdowns, completed 79.4 percent of his passes, and had a 131.5 passer rating, the third-highest total of his career at the time. Jones set career highs in catches (eight) and yards (123). And as a team the Packers rushed for 138 yards, their second-highest total of the year.

"I think we had a good plan," said Rodgers, who had his highest passer rating of the season. "We just got into a flow early. I think I haven't played this kind of game really this season yet.

"I'm playing the way I feel like I'm capable of playing. It was nice to play better. It was obviously a combination of a number of things, but (coach) Mike (McCarthy) called some very high-percentage plays early in the game for me, and I feel like I really got into a rhythm early."

Following the game, Cowboys owner Jerry Jones relieved head coach Wade Phillips of his duties. It was the first of back-to-back games the Packers sent a head coach to the unemployment line.

Green Bay was heading to its bye week with a 6–3 record and a three-game winning streak. The first stretch of the season was far more challenging than anyone would have imagined, but somehow, Rodgers and the Packers had survived.

"It gives us momentum going into the bye week," Woodson said of the dominant win. "We have some time off, which slows us down a little bit, but hopefully we come back in a couple weeks ready to go, and have that same intensity."

They did.

In its first game after the bye week, Green Bay went to Minnesota to face a Vikings team on the brink of collapse. By the time things had ended, Minnesota had undoubtedly crumbled.

The Packers buried the Vikings 31–3, and I remember my broadcast partner Larry McCarren marveling over how much the Packers had improved in the three weeks since they escaped Lambeau with a tense victory over the Vikings.

Rodgers was virtually flawless, throwing for 301 yards and four touchdowns—including three to Greg Jennings. Favre had another rough day as the Packers routed their border-state rivals by 28 points.

Oh, and by the way, the Vikings fired head coach Brad Childress after that game.

The Packers went to Atlanta on Thanksgiving weekend for a showdown with the high-flying Falcons. The Packers' trip to the Georgia Dome didn't go as planned, as Atlanta's Matt Bryant kicked a 47-yard field goal with just 9 seconds left and the Falcons prevailed 20–17.

There was no shame in losing a game like that on the road to the team with the best record in the NFC. Many of us figured we'd see a Packers–Falcons game in January, but now it was more likely to be in Atlanta instead of Green Bay.

"I have no plans of going to Lambeau Field in January," Falcons wideout Roddy White said. "I plan on staying right here and sleeping in my own bed in the playoffs."

The Packers handled the 49ers in Green Bay the following week with veteran wide receiver Donald Driver turning back the clock during a remarkable 61-yard catch-and-run touchdown.

On Green Bay's opening drive of the second half and the Packers facing a second-and-16 at their own 39, Driver lined up in the right slot. Driver found a hole in San Francisco's zone and hauled in a strike from Rodgers at the 49ers' 38.

Driver spun away from safety Reggie Smith at the 30, then ducked under a tackle attempt by safety Dashon Goldson at the 22. Cornerback Nate Clements had an angle on Driver, but Driver simply shoved him out of the way at the 10.

Three 49ers finally corralled Driver at the 4, but he dragged them into the right corner of the end zone for an improbable 61-yard touchdown and a 21–13 Green Bay lead.

When Driver reached the end zone, I remember exclaiming, "The old man's still got it!" on the radio.

"Donald made one of the most amazing catches and runs I've ever seen," Rodgers said. "We nicknamed him 'the Kickstand.' That's been his nickname around here since I've been here. When he was at about the 20 I was thinking, 'Go down, go down, don't get drilled,' and then when he broke another tackle I was hoping he'd get it in the end zone."

Costly Defeat

The Packers were 8–4 with five wins in their last six games. They appeared to have survived the tough overtime losses and the plethora of injuries and looked like they were about to become the team everyone thought they'd be at the outset of the season.

We were in Detroit in Week 14 in mid-December. I distinctly remember that head coach Mike McCarthy was very relaxed that morning as we sat down to do our pregame interview at Ford Field. No one saw what was coming that afternoon.

Rodgers and the offense struggled through a scoreless first quarter without a first down. Late in the second quarter, Rodgers took off on an 18-yard scramble that appeared to be the spark the offense needed.

Rodgers was slow getting up from the tackle. The Packers took a timeout and then Rodgers was sacked on the next play. Rodgers had suffered a concussion that not only cost the Packers in the 7–3 loss to the Lions, but would cost him the next week, as well.

After the game, I remember McCarthy being as upset with his team as he was relaxed prior to the game. The Lions were by no means a juggernaut, finishing that season just 6–10.

And with or without Rodgers, the Packers' offense had to produce more than three points because the defense played well enough to win.

The Packers were 8–5, and if the playoffs had begun that day, they would not have qualified for the field.

Confidence Boost

The next day, following the Lions debacle, McCarthy sensed that perhaps the long season and the even longer list of injuries were taking a toll on the locker room.

McCarthy might have sensed a little doubt creeping into the psyche of his players and he had to address it.

The Packers faced a huge Sunday-night game on the road in New England against the best team in the AFC. It seemed like the Patriots hadn't lost at home since Paul Revere made his historic ride.

That week, McCarthy announced to his team that Rodgers would not be playing due to a concussion he suffered in Detroit. He also told his squad to keep that piece of information to themselves for competitive reasons. McCarthy wanted to make the Patriots prepare for Rodgers, even though he wasn't going to play. That's how coaches think.

I'm sure McCarthy saw the look on the faces of his players. For weeks, all anyone on the outside talked about were the mounting injuries. But the team always felt they still had a chance if No. 12 suited up.

Well, now Rodgers wasn't going to play and McCarthy wanted to make sure his players believed they could still win. McCarthy then said, in a rather angry tone, "We're nobody's underdogs!"

But McCarthy knew that actions speak louder than words, especially to professional athletes. So McCarthy declared, "If we win the toss we are going to defer." After pausing for effect, McCarthy said "Then we are going to onside kick, recover it, and score. We're going to dictate the flow of this game!"

Now the room had to be looking at their head coach and wondering, "Is this guy nuts?" But they also had to think, "This guy believes in us and he's proving it."

If the players had any doubt at that point in the season it began to recede. It was replaced by a quiet confidence instilled by the actions of their head coach that would carry them to New England and beyond.

That Sunday, on the way from the team hotel to Foxboro, I was in a carpool that included our statistician, Tom Hecker; Carl Moll, the director of the Packers Radio Network; and Larry McCarren, my partner on the radio. We were listening to the New York Giants and Philadelphia Eagles wrapping up their game at the Meadowlands.

Eagles return man DeSean Jackson returned a punt 65 yards for a touchdown in the final seconds to win the game. Little did we know at the time how significant that result would be. Without Jackson's return to beat the Giants, the Packers would not have made the playoffs that year.

Later that night, McCarthy's plan unfolded to perfection. The Packers won the toss, deferred, and executed a perfect onside kick that was recovered by safety Nick Collins. The Packers used the first six-plus minutes of the quarter to run 11 plays, covering 40 yards and resulting in a 31-yard Mason Crosby field goal.

Even though all Green Bay managed was a field goal, the intended tone had been set. The Packers were not going to play like some patsies.

New England responded with a seven-play, 73-yard drive to take a 7–3 lead. On the first play of the second quarter, backup quarterback Matt Flynn hit James Jones on a 66-yard touchdown pass and it was "game on."

The Packers added another touchdown on a long 82-yard drive that ate up 6:26. That gave the Packers a 17–7 advantage with just more than two minutes to go in the first half.

Then the inexplicable happened. On Crosby's ensuing kickoff, a squib kick to run out the clock, 313-pound New England offensive lineman Dan Connolly picked up the ball and proceeded to rumble 71 yards. That return set up a short Tom Brady-to-Aaron Hernandez touchdown pass just before halftime, cutting the Packers' advantage to 17–14.

Nonetheless, Green Bay had to feel good about its standing at halftime. The Packers were the aggressor, they were dictating the flow of the game, and with each passing moment you could see the confidence growing in that young Green Bay team.

The Packers held a 27–21 lead early in the fourth quarter when Brady and the Patriots put together two scoring drives to take a 31–27 lead. But the Packers weren't going anywhere. Green Bay carried the battle right down to the end.

Flynn drove Green Bay from its own 43-yard line to the New England 15, where on fourth-and-1 he was sacked and fumbled. The Patriots recovered and the Packers were heading home following a 31–27 defeat that left them with an 8–6 record.

Despite the defeat, the Packers left Foxboro that night fully believing in themselves once again. If they could go blow for blow with arguably football's best team—and do it without Rodgers—they could play with anybody, right?

"I think that was a huge point in our season for our confidence," Driver said. "We didn't win the game. But after that game, we knew we could play with anybody again."

I don't know how to say this any other way, but there are *no* moral victories in pro sports. The losing team does not get a juice box at the end of the game! Everybody doesn't get a trophy.

Teams don't usually gain confidence through defeat. On the professional level, it is all about winning. Well, none of that pertained to the Green Bay Packers that December night in 2010.

On the plane ride back from New England I could sense a palpable feeling of confidence from the Packers players. They did everything that night except win the game. McCarthy's plan had worked. His actions that week, the way he prepared his team and handled the game, instilled in his players the confidence they would need the rest of the season.

Green Bay took on the best team in the NFL in their house and played them right down to the wire without its starting quarterback! These Packers, minus all of the injured starters, realized that night in Foxboro that they could attain all of their goals.

In Their Hands

O n the way home from Foxboro, the Packers found out that they would make the playoffs by winning their final two games. So despite the two-game losing streak and an 8–6 record, the Packers were still in control of their own destiny if they could notch home wins against the New York Giants and Chicago.

The week before the Giants game, I had a conversation with Rodgers and he mentioned that being held out of the Patriots game was a blessing in disguise.

"I feel rested and stronger," he said.

The long grind of any season takes its toll on players, not just physically but mentally. We always hear from the old-timers—and I'm guilty of this as much as anyone—"How can these guys be tired?" They do very little hitting in practice.

Well, the mental aspect of today's game—the classroom work, attention to detail, having every moment of the day planned—is every bit as demanding as the physical.

I've seen teams, especially Mike Sherman's teams, come out of training camp tired and drained and not because they spent five weeks physically beating on each other. They were tired from the daily mental demands that today's game requires. Rodgers may have been suffering from fatigue late that season, but the week off rejuvenated him.

Rodgers and the Packers were on fire as they blistered the once-proud Giants defense with 515 yards of offense in a 45–17 blowout. Rodgers completed 25-of-37 passes for 404 yards and four touchdowns with no interceptions.

I guess he was right. That week off did him a lot of good!

"I felt all week a lot of energy," Rodgers said. "My arm felt like it was live. I threw the ball really good in practice, so I had a lot of confidence going into the game that I was going to perform this way—obviously, not maybe as well as it went—but I think you can contribute that to some really good play calls at certain times and some big plays by some guys."

For the Packers it was one down, with one to go to earn a postseason berth. That one to go was against their oldest rival, the Chicago Bears.

Chicago had clinched the NFC North and the No. 2 seed in the upcoming playoffs, and had nothing tangible to play for in Green Bay on the final week of the regular season. Most in Chicago believed the Bears would rest their starters in a contest that had little consequence for them.

But Bears head coach Lovie Smith insisted Chicago had a lot on the line that day.

First off, in deference to the Bears–Packers rivalry, Smith felt a duty to go "all in." Secondly, he knew the one club he did not want to see in the postseason was Green Bay. So the Bears were all in knowing a sweep of the Packers that season would prevent Green Bay from getting into the 2010 playoffs.

As brilliant as Rodgers and the high-flying Green Bay offense had been the week before against the Giants, the rugged Chicago defense brought them right back down to earth. The Packers trailed 3–0 at halftime and didn't reach the scoreboard until Mason Crosby kicked a 23-yard field goal with 2:39 to go in the third quarter to tie the game.

Green Bay took the lead on a one-yard touchdown pass from Rodgers to tight end Donald Lee with 12:42 to go in the game. A tense conclusion ensued with Green Bay's playoff hopes hanging in the balance.

Chicago had three possessions after the Packers took their seven-point lead. On the third of those drives, the Bears motored from their 12-yard line all the way to the Green Bay 32 in 14 plays.

With 20 seconds remaining, Chicago quarterback Jay Cutler threw a pass that was intercepted by Nick Collins. The dagger had been delivered, and with a 10–3 win in their pocket, the Packers were playoff bound.

"It feels incredible," said Packers outside linebacker Erik Walden, who had a career night with three sacks and 12 tackles. "It didn't always look great for us, but we got it done."

The Packers defense was dominant from start to finish. Dom Capers' unit sacked Cutler six times while limiting the Bears to 227 yards of offense and just three points.

"I don't know if it was our best [defensive] game this year or not," Packers nose tackle B.J. Raji said. "But if it wasn't, it was close."

What gets lost in the history of the 2010 Packers season is the brilliant clutch play of the defense throughout the year. If there is a difference between the 2010 defense and the defenses since in Green Bay, it's that when the offense struggled during that "super" season, the defense was capable of securing the win.

The Bears game and the 9–0 victory earlier that season at the New York Jets were won largely by the defense. Now, with the playoffs looming, the Packers defense would be a subtle key to their eventual success.

After the game, as the coaches met at midfield, McCarthy said to Smith, "Congratulations on the division title." And Smith said to McCarthy, "Congratulations on the win, and we'll see you in a few weeks."

That's a big part of the reason Chicago's head coach went all in. He knew his worst fears could come true if the Packers made the playoffs.

"I kept thinking we're going to see them again," Bears cornerback Tim Jennings said of the Packers. "I was thinking, 'Man, we should have knocked them out.'"

Postseason

Personally, I had my doubts about this Packers team making a deep postseason run. I looked at the injured reserve list and saw the names of a significant number of starters, and that's never a good thing in the playoffs. However, in almost every case where a starter went down in 2010, the next man up played even better!

Bryan Bulaga replaced Mark Tauscher at right tackle and had a terrific rookie season. Desmond Bishop had a huge year subbing for Nick Barnett. Running back James Starks was about to burst on the scene in place of Ryan Grant. The only player the Packers were not able to adequately replace with a better player was tight end Jermichael Finley.

This was remarkable, because that type of improved production almost never happens in the NFL! There is no doubt general manager Ted Thompson had built one of the deepest teams in the NFL. That depth not only got the Packers into the playoffs, but it would have to carry them in the postseason ahead.

The Packers were the last team to qualify for the playoffs in 2010, and I kept remembering back to the wardrobe statement made by the players at the Welcome Home luncheon prior to the season opener. After all of the injuries and the two early-season overtime losses, after six losses in all, this Packers team still had everything they wanted right in front of them.

But as the No. 6 seed in the NFC, they would not play at home again.

The playoff schedule did the Packers no favors. Remember that prior to the season opener, Green Bay had not won a game in Philadelphia in 48 years. Well, in 2010, the Packers would have to win twice in the City of Brotherly Love—in the regular season opener and now in the wild-card round.

The NFC playoffs opened with 7–9 Seattle ousting the defending Super Bowl Champion New Orleans Saints 41–36 on a Saturday evening. The highlight came via a 67-yard Marshawn Lynch run for the ages.

One major contender was out of the picture, but the Packers had work to do in Philly the next day.

Since the Packers knocked out Eagles starting quarterback Kevin Kolb in the season opener, Michael Vick came on and shined. Overall, Vick had the best season of his career in 2010.

Vick finished second to Rodgers in the NFC in passer rating (100.2). Vick threw for 3,018 yards with 21 touchdowns and just six interceptions. He also rushed for 676 yards and nine touchdowns, and was named the starter for the NFC in the Pro Bowl.

Rodgers had never won a playoff game, while Vick was a veteran and just the kind of talent that could give the Packers defense fits. The Eagles were favored at home, but the Packers came out blazing and built a 14–3 lead by halftime.

Green Bay added a running element to its potent offense as James Starks rushed for 123 yards on 23 carries. Rodgers also threw three touchdown passes, and the Packers played on the lead all day.

Of course, Vick brought the Eagles back in the second half. And with the game on the line in the final seconds, he drove Philadelphia to the Green Bay 27-yard line.

On first-and-10, Vick faked a throw down the middle, then threw for rookie Riley Cooper in the left corner of the end zone. Tramon Williams never bit on the ball fake, though, and had perfect position to intercept Vick's pass with 33 seconds left, giving the Packers a 21–16 win and sending them to the NFC Divisional playoffs.

"I feel like I got greedy and took a shot at the end zone," Vick said. "I didn't throw the ball I wanted and got picked. It's not the way I wanted to go out, but I went down swinging."

It helped that Eagles All-Pro kicker David Akers missed field goals of 41 and 34 yards that day, but style points don't matter in the playoffs. All that matters is win and advance.

How far was this Packers team going to go in the postseason?

Could this group become "super?"

We got our answer the following Saturday night in the divisional round against the top-seeded Atlanta Falcons.

Becoming Super

The Packers returned to Atlanta where the Falcons had defeated them 20–17 in late November. The NFC Divisional playoff game was also a rematch of two of the league's best young quarterbacks in Aaron Rodgers and Matt Ryan.

Atlanta earned the No. 1 seed in the playoffs by virtue of its 13–3 record. The game was played inside the Georgia Dome, and it was rocking after Eric Weems took a kickoff back 102 yards for a touchdown and a 14–7 Atlanta lead with less than 12 minutes to go in the second quarter.

What happened in those last 11 minutes, 50 seconds of that quarter is where I believe the Packers became "super." Undaunted by the noise or the kickoff return, Rodgers led the Packers on a 92-yard drive in 10 plays, culminating with fullback John Kuhn plunging into the end zone from one yard out to tie the game at 14–14.

On Green Bay's next possession, Rodgers led an 80-yard, seven-play march, hitting James Jones on a beautiful corner route, and the Packers had a 21–14 lead.

With the half winding down, the Falcons were just trying to get into field-goal range and pull within four points. Williams, who had a memorable 2010 postseason, had different ideas.

The biggest play of the game was arguably the final one of the first half. Green Bay had taken a 21–14 lead, but Atlanta was driving into field goal range and had reached the Packers' 35.

With just 10 seconds left in the half, Ryan rolled left and threw back against his body for Roddy White. Williams jumped the route, though, made a nifty cut past Ryan at midfield, then sailed to the end zone to make it 28–14 as time expired.

On Atlanta's previous possession, Ryan took a shot to the end zone for 6'4" wideout Michael Jenkins. But the 5'11" Williams played the ball better, and when Jenkins lost his footing, Williams went up and picked Ryan off.

In the matter of two short minutes, Williams completely changed the football game with two enormous interceptions.

"I think everything he's done, every good thing that's happened to Tramon on the field, all the plays he's making he deserves," Packers linebacker A.J. Hawk said of Williams. "I've never been around probably a better teammate than a guy like Tramon. He's awesome. I love how he prepares. He does everything right."

The Packers had trailed 14–7 with 12 minutes left in the half. Green Bay then scored 21 unanswered points.

"I think we have lots of guys on the defense that can make those plays," Williams said. "I think I've just been put in that position the last couple of weeks and made those plays from my teammates. I don't see it as a big deal."

It was a huge deal. Amazingly, Rodgers was an even bigger deal.

Rodgers, making just his third postseason start, had a game for the ages in the Georgia Dome. He completed 31-of-36 passes for 366 yards, three touchdowns, and no interceptions, and posted a passer rating of 136.8.

His performance against Atlanta was arguably the greatest postseason game ever by a Packers quarterback and one of the finest in NFL history.

Rodgers set Packers playoff records for completions (31) and completion percentage (86.1 percent), and had the second-most passing yardage in team history (366). In 10 possessions, Rodgers led Green Bay to five touchdowns and two field goals, and the Packers never punted.

The signal-caller threw touchdown passes to Jordy Nelson (six yards), James Jones (20 yards), and John Kuhn (seven yards). Rodgers was razor-sharp, shredded what had been a respectable defense, and got plenty of help from his gifted wideouts.

The most impressive part of Rodgers' day, though, might have been his feet. On several plays, Atlanta standout defensive end John Abraham seemed ready to dump Rodgers. But the nifty quarterback escaped and even had a seven-yard touchdown run.

"This probably was my best performance—the stage we were on, the importance of this game," Rodgers said afterward. "It was a good night."

To say the least.

Green Bay went on to rout the top-seeded Falcons 48–21. I remember David Archer, the former Falcons quarterback now working as the analyst on the Falcons radio network, coming over to our booth and saying, "Congratulations; you've got a great team there."

I remarked to Larry McCarren, then the sports director of WFRV-TV in Green Bay, that he had better clear his schedule for the next three weeks because the Packers were going to the Super Bowl!

The next day, Chicago rolled past Seattle 35–24. Now, one of the most anticipated NFC Championship games in league history was set.

The NFL's oldest rivals would meet at Soldier Field for the right to represent the conference in Super Bowl XLV.

"Personally, I'm honored to be a part of this and to be going down to Soldier Field to play for the Halas trophy and for the opportunity to play for the Lombardi trophy," McCarthy said. "It speaks volumes. It's great for both organizations, great for our fans. It's going to be a fun game to play in."

Epic Championship Matchup

There's an old saying: "Familiarity breeds contempt." In the case of the Packers and Bears, the two "primeval enemies"—a description penned by former Packers public relations director Lee Remmel years ago—of the "black and blue" NFC North Division, familiarity certainly breeds contempt and it often produces less-than-pretty football.

I guess that's to be expected. I don't think there is anything one team could do that the other side hasn't seen. So it becomes a grind-it-out, who-wants-it-more affair.

Coming off their exhilarating victory at Atlanta the week before, the Packers took the opening kickoff and put together an impressive 84-yard touchdown drive. Rodgers capped the march with a one-yard touchdown run around the left end of the offensive line.

"Frankly, the first drive was the way we anticipated coming into this game," McCarthy said. "I thought we were able to get into a tremendous rhythm."

In the second quarter James Starks capped a relatively short five-play, 44-yard drive with a four-yard touchdown run. The Packers led 14–0 at the half, and Green Bay's defense was in command, holding the struggling Bears offense to just 103 yards and 0-for-5 on third downs.

In the third quarter, Chicago lost quarterback Jay Cutler to a knee injury. His replacement, veteran Todd Collins, lasted two ineffective series and was replaced by third-stringer Caleb Hanie late in the third quarter.

The Packers defense had prepared all week for Cutler. They spent a short amount of time getting ready for Collins.

Caleb Hanie?

"We didn't even know who their third-string quarterback was," Packers defensive end Ryan Pickett said. "We [were] like, 'Who is that?'"

The Packers would soon find out.

With just more than nine minutes to go in the third quarter, Rodgers drove the Packers to the Chicago 6-yard line. What he did next was inexplicable. Rodgers threw a red-zone interception.

Bears Pro Bowl linebacker Brian Urlacher picked Rodgers off and returned the errant pass up the west sideline with just one man to beat.

That one man was the author of the interception, and he described the sequence as "one of the few good plays I made all day."

Rodgers dove at Urlacher's ankles and brought him down at the Chicago 45-yard line. Green Bay's defense turned Chicago away, though, and from there, with Collins replacing Cutler, the Packers escaped trouble.

However, still trailing 14–0 at the end of the third quarter, the Bears rallied under Hanie. The third-stringer engineered an eight-play, 67-yard drive that Chester Taylor capped with a one-yard touchdown run that pulled the Bears within seven.

With the Packers clinging to that 14–7 lead midway through the fourth quarter, defensive tackle B.J. Raji made a play that McCarthy called a "game-winner."

The Bears had a third-and-5 from their own 15. Raji lined up over center Olin Kreutz, showed blitz, then dropped into the middle of the field where Hanie was trying to get the ball to running back Matt Forte.

Hanie never saw Raji and threw the ball right into his enormous mitts. Raji caught the ball naturally, then waltzed to the right corner of the end zone for an 18-yard touchdown that gave Green Bay a 21–7 lead. Raji didn't have an interception in the NFL or college, so his timing was ideal for Packer Nation.

"It's just a great feeling," Raji said. "It was a great call. I was behind the back and obviously he wasn't expecting that. I just caught it and ran it back."

I declared on the radio, "An NFC Championship dagger!" Many felt that was a bit premature. My thought was, if your nose tackle intercepts their third-string quarterback and scores a touchdown, giving you a 21–7 lead with just more than six minutes remaining, and it isn't your day, then it never will be your day. Fortunately for the Packers, it was their day—but not without a few anxious moments.

Now, who on that beautiful 20-degree sunny Sunday afternoon

would have thought someone named Caleb Hanie would mount the Bears' comeback in the NFC Championship game? Even better, how many Bears fans even knew Caleb Hanie was on the roster?

Hanie, who was undrafted coming out of Colorado State in 2008, had thrown just 14 career passes and entered with a passer rating of 39.6. Amazingly, he almost led the Bears back from the abyss.

But there he was, undaunted by the Raji interception. Hanie hit Earl Bennett with a 35-yard touchdown pass, capping an alarmingly quick four-play, 60-yard drive that took just 1:21 off the clock.

"I ain't going to lie, when they put him in we [were] like, 'We don't know [anything] about this guy,'" Packers defensive end Cullen Jenkins said. "But he did great."

The Bears forced a Green Bay punt and got the ball back with 2:53 to go. Hanie drove Chicago to the Green Bay 29-yard line with 47 seconds remaining.

I remember saying to Larry on the air, "If Caleb Hanie gets this game into overtime, they will canonize him in five different religions." Larry said, "Name four."

Well, there was no canonization that day in any religion at Soldier Field. Hanie's next pass was intercepted by rookie Sam Shields, his second theft of the game.

Finally, the long, tense fourth quarter was over. Green Bay had escaped with a 21–14 win.

The Packers were headed to Super Bowl XLV.

"I'm numb. It's a great feeling," McCarthy said. "I'm just so proud of our football team.

"Defense, special teams, people making plays down the stretch. It was the typical Green Bay–Chicago game with everything on the line. I'm very proud of our players and very proud of our coaches. As we stated, we have a goal of playing 16 quarters and we've completed 12. We're fired up and getting ready to go to Dallas, Texas."

One Mind, One Heartbeat, One Goal, One Game

After the game, I felt happiest for three people.

One was Rodgers, who was now emerging from the shadow of Favre. After an ugly training camp in 2008 and two losses to Favre and the Vikings in 2009, Rodgers had emerged as an elite quarterback.

Another was Donald Driver, who came to Green Bay in the seventh round of the 1999 draft and was now the Packers' second all-time leading receiver. Driver had come further than anyone on the roster, and was now headed to his first-ever Super Bowl.

And the third was Charles Woodson, who had done just about everything in his career, including playing and losing in a Super Bowl, while with the Raiders. Woodson was carving out a Hall of Fame career. Now, he was one win from becoming a Super Bowl champion.

Woodson stood on top of a table in the victorious Packers' locker room that late afternoon in Chicago. He then set the tone for the next two weeks with his now-famous speech to his teammates.

"I want y'all to think about one thing—one. For two weeks, think about one. Let's be one mind, let's be one heartbeat, for one purpose, one goal, for one more game—one.

"Let's get it. And check this, if the President doesn't want to come watch us in the Super Bowl, guess what? We'll go see him! Let's get a 'White House' on three. One-Two-Three [collectively] 'White House!'"

So profound was that moment that part of Woodson's speech—"one mind, one goal, one purpose, one heart"—is inscribed on the inside of the Packers' Super Bowl XLV championship ring. But I'm getting ahead of myself. The Packers had two weeks to prepare for a veteran Pittsburgh Steelers team, whose core had been part of championships in Super Bowl XL and XLIII.

In the first week of the two-week run-up to the big game, Super Bowl teams try to take care of the rudimentary business of family, tickets, logistics, etc. They also put in the major portion of their preparation for the game itself at home during practice.

By the time they hit the road to the "super" city, the game plan has been crafted. And the week of on-site practices involves just adjustments and polish. McCarthy kept telling his young team, "Trust your preparation."

Super Bowl Week

I arrived in Dallas Monday night of Super Bowl week. I had been in Denver working on a project, and flew in separately from the team. I will never forget the turbulence we experienced coming into DFW. There was a major weather front moving into the Dallas area and the airliner was getting tossed around like a Wiffle ball.

We arrived safely and I got to the media hotel in downtown Dallas late that evening. When I woke up the next day, the front had moved through and deposited an inch and a half of ice over the entire Dallas metro area.

They are not prepared for this type of weather in that part of the country, and the entire metroplex was paralyzed. They had reportedly just a handful of snowplows and the only salt they had in the area was used for margaritas, not icy streets!

I thought media day would be postponed but in front of our hotel were four buses ready to go. They were taking people from the hotel out to AT&T Stadium for Super Bowl Media Day. No one but these buses dared going on the freeways that day. I just marveled that not even God could stop NFL media day at the Super Bowl!

Green Bay's inexperience on such an enormous stage was a major topic.

The Packers hadn't played in a Super Bowl in 13 years, when they lost a heartbreaker to Denver 31–24. And the only 2010–11 Packers to ever have played in a Super Bowl were Woodson and Pickett, who both played on losing teams.

My family on Super Bowl Sunday. From left are son Bryan, daughter-in-law Rachel, son Scott, and my wife, Julie. It was special to share the super experience with them.

Pittsburgh, meanwhile, had 14 starters who had won a Super Bowl. The Steelers had 10 players with two rings, and a total of 25 players who had competed in a Super Bowl.

The Packers were hopeful that component wouldn't play a major role in deciding the outcome of Super Bowl XLV.

"I believe if we stay calm and stay cool and understand what's going on, everything will work out," Packers running back Brandon Jackson said. "We've been on the big stage before, not as big as this, but as far as playoffs and everything like that, we've been on that type of stage. We're going to handle our business, stay calm and cool, and everything will work out."

Many Packers admitted that Pittsburgh's experience might be beneficial during the days leading up to Super Bowl XLV. But the Packers were optimistic that once game time arrived, the Steelers' experience wouldn't matter much.

"I think the only advantage they have on us is getting through the week and dealing with the distractions," fullback John Kuhn said. "They will have experienced that before and they know how to play that game. We are well aware of that and we know the advantage they might have in the distraction game.

"But when we get into the game, then it's just the Super Bowl. Then it's just a football game. We've all experienced plenty of football games, but it's the event around the Super Bowl that nobody has experienced."

The biggest distraction Green Bay faced was with its official Super Bowl team photo.

The Packers were originally scheduled to take their team picture on the Tuesday of Super Bowl week. Green Bay's 15 players on injured reserve weren't arriving until Thursday, though.

That meant the injured players would be left out of the shot. So players such as linebacker Nick Barnett and tight end Jermichael Finley took to Twitter to voice their displeasure.

"It's kinda sad," Barnett wrote.

"We got hurt playing for the team," Finley tweeted. "I never trip abt anything, but the way IR players are getting treated…I guess its what have u done for me lately!"

Rodgers has this observation when he shot back at his injured teammates.

"I was on IR back in 2006," Rodgers said. "I chose to stick around and finish out the season with my guys and be here every game. Some of those guys didn't. And so, we love them, we care about them, we don't wish injury on anybody, but this is a group of guys that's really come together and has been great to work with. Some of the guys who were injured, you know, they are still part of this team, but some of them didn't choose to stick around."

McCarthy called the entire situation "a total overreaction," which it was. He then settled it all by moving the team picture to Friday, when the entire team could be present.

"If that's the biggest issue that we have in our preparation, we are going to have a hell of a week," McCarthy said. "So it's not that big of a deal."

The weather continued to be cold all week and people, including my family, were struggling to get into Dallas. Even "Radio Row" at the media hotel was quiet until late Thursday and Friday. Visitors simply couldn't get into the area. Fortunately, the two teams had arrived ahead of the storm.

My family did get into town late Friday evening. My wife, Julie, son Scott, and daughter-in-law, Rachel, persevered through several delays and finally made it. My other son, Bryan, was coming in from Los Angeles for the game and flew into Love Field on Saturday. Believe me, having them there for this game was special.

Twenty-five years earlier at Super Bowl XX, my previous and only Super Bowl, my son Scott was too young to go to the game. My youngest son, Bryan, had not even been born yet.

Bryan had been my longtime spotter for Packers games in Green Bay. A spotter's job in a broadcast is to point out on my roster boards whom he sees making the tackle, intercepting a pass, or picking up a fumble—a very necessary job in a football broadcast.

Bryan was just starting middle school when we moved from Chicago to Milwaukee. He began working with me on the games in the 1999 season. He spotted for us right through college and then moved to the West Coast for work. I am indebted to my boss and friend Carl Moll, the director of the Packers Radio Network, for allowing Bryan to come back and work with us on the NFC Championship Game and Super Bowl following the 2010 season. Being able to work those games together made the experience all the more special for me and I know for Bryan, as well. That put a nice bow on his Packers experience in our booth.

Super Bowl XLV for me was the culmination of why I came to Green Bay. Most of us in sports are, or were, fans. If you are a real fan, you pick a team in childhood and you stay with that team or those teams the rest of your life.

I grew up in Western Massachusetts in the 1960s and 70s. I was about five or six years old when I started to follow the New York Yankees in baseball (at the behest of my grandfather) and the Green Bay Packers in football. My favorite colors were green and gold and I thought the "G" on the side of the Packers' helmet was absolutely the most unique insignia I had ever seen.

I really liked the look of the navy blue interlocked "NY" on the pinstripes of the Yankees' uniform. You see—even back then, sports marketing was at work. I had a lunch pail in sixth grade with Jim Taylor on the front in his green-and-gold jersey, the No. 31 emblazoned across the front and that cool gold helmet. I don't know what happened to the lunch pail, but I would pay good money to get it back!

As a kid I remember broadcasting Packers games in my head with Bart Starr and the Lombardi teams. The Ice Bowl captured my imagination like no other game—even to this day. I always felt that once I got into this business, if I ever got the chance to broadcast for one of my childhood teams, it would be about as good as it gets. To broadcast a Super Bowl for that team would be the highlight of my career!

Psychology Professor

I mentioned earlier that McCarthy had used some interesting motivational tactics that season, helping to spur his team along the way.

He hung a blank frame on the wall of the team room and said, "Our picture is going there, next to the 12 other Green Bay title teams, when we win the championship."

McCarthy expressed supreme confidence in New England when he carried out on his promise to defer, onside kick, recover, score, and dictate the tempo of that game all night.

Now, on the eve of the Super Bowl, McCarthy was looking for something to again instill confidence in his young team in its biggest hour. McCarthy felt better than ever about his team—so good, in fact, that he pulled a stunner less than 24 hours before the game.

On Saturday night, McCarthy made the bold move of fitting his players for the championship rings.

Traditionally, teams get fitted after winning a title. But the McCarthy Way was now much different from many of his peers.

The Packers' confidence was sky high. And this only added to it.

"That's pretty much how he coached us all year, and especially at the end," Pickett said. "He had a lot of confidence in us and we had a lot of confidence in each other."

Cornerback Charles Woodson agreed.

"No matter what anyone said about him he never changed his focus on getting to this point," Woodson said of McCarthy. "When you have a coach who is unwavered by whatever is going on in the media or whatever is said about him, you know that you have a good guy at the helm. We followed him and his lead and here we are with a chance to win the Super Bowl."

Super Sunday

There was nothing easy about working this Super Bowl, because everything and everyone was roughly 45 minutes away in that huge metropolitan area. The Packers were in one area; the Steelers in another. The stadium wasn't close to either team; Dallas was downtown; and Fort Worth was the party town.

We took the shuttle to the stadium almost six hours before kickoff on Super Bowl Sunday due to travel, traffic, security, and everything else involved in an event of this size.

The Super Bowl that year matched two of the most beloved teams in the league and two of the most energetic fan bases. That made this Super Bowl crowd a little different from the typical corporate in-house audience for the championship game. The "real" fans somehow got into this game, and they made it an electric atmosphere all afternoon and evening.

Early in the game, it was apparent the two best players on Pittsburgh's roster were not quite 100 percent. Quarterback Ben Roethlisberger was erratic, in particular when he missed wideout Antonio Brown, who was wide open on a third-and-10 pass at the Steelers' 49-yard line to end the first offensive series of the day.

Roethlisberger had reportedly sustained a thigh injury earlier in the playoffs and maybe that leg injury led to some inconsistency in is game. At times he looked sharp. At others, he was inexplicably inaccurate. Roethlisberger finished the day 25-of-40 for 263 yards, two touchdowns, and two interceptions, and posted a 77.4 passer rating. It was not his finest hour.

Meanwhile, All-Pro safety Troy Polamalu, who was the NFL's Defensive Player of the Year that season, seemed a half step slow on several occasions due to an Achilles-related injury that had bothered him late in the season and forced him to sit out a couple of games. The Packers took advantage of Polamalu, just barely beating the Steelers great on numerous occasions.

Rodgers was extremely sharp on this day. Time and again, he put the ball exactly where it needed to be—often threading the needle just beyond the reach of a Pittsburgh defender.

Rodgers was as crisp as a quarterback could be, and his 304 passing yards might have been 450 if it wasn't for several dropped passes by Green Bay's receivers. His passer rating of 111.5 was the fourth-highest in Super Bowl history at the time.

Most importantly, though, Rodgers was terrific in taking care of the ball. He threw three touchdown passes, didn't have an interception or fumble, and was an easy choice for MVP.

Super Strategy

The Steelers brought the No. 1 rushing defense into Super Bowl XLV. Pittsburgh allowed just 62.8 yards rushing per game and only three yards per attempt.

Mike McCarthy had James Starks cranked up and running well, as the rookie back averaged 87.7 yards per game in his three playoff outings. On this day, though, against the dominant Pittsburgh run defense, McCarthy's Packers ran the ball all of 13 times!

McCarthy built his offensive game plan around Rodgers, who had shredded these same Steelers just 14 months earlier during a 37–36 loss in Pittsburgh. McCarthy loved the matchups of his receivers against Pittsburgh's secondary, and now it was up to Green Bay's line to protect and for Rodgers to deliver.

"A huge part of our game plan was really putting the ball in Aaron Rodgers' hands," McCarthy said.

As McCarthy & Co. studied the Steelers, they saw that other teams had defeated them thanks to efficient aerial attacks.

In Week 7, New Orleans downed Pittsburgh 20–10, and quarterback Drew Brees threw for 305 yards and posted a passer rating of 101.0. Two weeks later, New England downed the Steelers 39–26 when Tom Brady threw for 350 yards and had a rating of 117.4.

The Packers took those performances and factored them into their blueprint for how to beat the Pittsburgh defense. Green Bay was going to win or lose this game doing what it does best—throw the football.

It proved to be the right strategy, especially with the way Rodgers played that day.

All Green Early

On Green Bay's second possession of a scoreless game, Rodgers went to work on the Steelers secondary. Sharp, accurate, and rhythmic,

Rodgers hooked up twice with wideout Jordy Nelson for 18 total yards and brilliantly avoided pressure to find Brandon Jackson for 14 yards.

The Packers had driven to the Steelers' 29-yard line when, on third-and-1, they lined up with two tight ends and Nelson, the lone receiver, split far right. Pittsburgh anticipated a run, and that left Nelson one-on-one with mediocre cornerback William Gay.

Gay came to the line to play press coverage, but Nelson beat him by faking inside, then releasing down the right sideline. The Packers offensive linemen did their jobs, and Rodgers lofted a perfect fade to the right corner of the end zone.

Nelson had a step on Gay and won a hand-fighting battle between the two. Nelson then hauled in Rodgers' gorgeous toss to give the Packers a 7–0 lead with 3:44 left in the first quarter.

"It was just press [coverage]," Nelson said." Aaron gave me a little signal if it was press to go deep. It was actually a screen play, but he checked to a go route. That's what we hit."

Green Bay's hitting had only begun.

Pittsburgh began its next drive on its own 7-yard line after an illegal block penalty on the kickoff. And on the first play, Roethlisberger made perhaps the game's biggest blunder.

Green Bay rushed just four, but Roethlisberger was trying to hit a home run to Mike Wallace so he needed substantial time for the play to develop. That allowed beefy defensive end Howard Green, who was signed off the street in October when the Packers were ravaged by injury, to get home.

Green whipped left guard Chris Kemoeatu, then drilled Roethlisberger as he let loose a bomb for Wallace. Green's pressure caused Roethlisberger's pass to be severely underthrown, and Packers safety Nick Collins intercepted the ball.

Collins, who was named to three straight Pro Bowls, took off down the right sideline and made a nifty cut back inside. When Collins got to the 3-yard line, he jumped and reached the end zone.

In a matter of 24 seconds, Green Bay had surged to a 14–0 lead.

"Oh man, that was the highlight of my day right there," Collins said. "I was able to read Big Ben [Roethlisberger] and got a nice jump on the ball. I made a couple cuts to get into the end zone."

The Steelers reached the board with a field goal in the second quarter, but the Packers responded.

With the Packers leading 14–3, Pittsburgh was on the move. Operating out of the shotgun, Roethlisberger threw a short pass over the middle for Wallace, but cornerback Jarrett Bush read the crossing route, drove on the ball, and picked it off.

Bush, one of the more maligned players in recent Packers history, developed into a special teams stalwart in 2010. But this was undoubtedly the biggest play he made from scrimmage during his five years in Green Bay.

"You know what, you've got to give them a lot of credit," Roethlisberger said. "They're a great defense; they got after us and I turned the ball over and you can't do that."

Especially with a quarterback like Rodgers on the other side.

Green Bay started on its own 47, and on its second play, Rodgers hit Nelson for 16 yards against nickel corner Bryant McFadden. Two plays later, Rodgers made one of his finest throws as a Packer.

On a first-and-10 from Pittsburgh's 21, the Packers lined up four wide receivers, while the Steelers rushed four and dropped seven. Greg Jennings lined up in the left slot and ran a deep seam route.

Jennings had gotten behind linebacker James Farrior and in front of safety Ryan Clark, but Rodgers' window was small and his pass had to be perfect. It was.

Rodgers delivered a dart that Clark missed by inches. Jennings took a wicked shot from safety Troy Polamalu, but he was already in the end zone.

The Packers led 21–3 with just more than two minutes remaining in the first half. Things couldn't be going any better.

"It was like they were a hair faster than we were all night," Clark said.

At the two-minute mark, cornerback Sam Shields left with a shoulder injury. Shields would return, but not until the fourth quarter.

One play later, cornerback Charles Woodson—Green Bay's best free agent since Reggie White—suffered a broken collarbone and wouldn't return. Earlier in that second quarter, wideout Donald Driver had left with an ankle injury and he wouldn't be back, either.

In a game that capped a season full of injuries for the Packers, why should the Super Bowl be any different?

With the Packers shorthanded and scrambling defensively on that final series of the first half, Pittsburgh took full advantage. Roethlisberger threw for all 77 yards of the drive—highlighted by an 8-yard touchdown to Hines Ward—and the Steelers pulled within 21–10 just 39 seconds before halftime.

During the 30-minute intermission, an emotionally distraught Woodson tried addressing his teammates.

"I was pretty emotional so I didn't get a whole lot out," Woodson said. "But just to tell them to get it done."

His message was heard.

"He could barely say much, he was very emotional and choked up," safety Charlie Peprah said of Woodson. "He got about three words out. He just said, 'You know how bad I want this,' and we knew what we had to do."

A Change of Momentum

With Woodson and Shields sidelined, Green Bay was searching for defensive answers. But the Packers didn't have any early in the third quarter.

After the Packers went three-and-out to start the half—a series that included a drop from James Jones that might have gone for a touchdown

This momentum stemming from a forced fumble by Clay Matthews and Ryan Pickett was the result of preparation and trust. (Jim Biever Photography)

—Pittsburgh took over at midfield. Five running plays later, the Steelers had gone 50 yards and Rashard Mendenhall was in the end zone.

Green Bay's lead, once as many as 18 points, had been whittled to 21–17. Pittsburgh radio play-by-play announcer Bill Hillgrove exclaimed on the Steelers broadcast, "This momentum change is profound!"

"It was tough," Packers defensive coordinator Dom Capers said. "We were scrambling there for a while, because a big part of our game plan went out the window. We planned on playing a lot of man coverage, and when those guys went out we had to become more of a zone team."

Green Bay's struggles continued. One series after Jones had a critical drop, Nelson had a drop of his own—one of his three on the day—leading to a Packers punt.

Green Bay's defense got a much-needed stop, but on its next

offensive series, Packers No. 5 wideout Brett Swain had a brutal drop. McCarthy challenged the play—and lost—and the Packers punted from deep in their territory.

At one point after a drop I exclaimed on the radio, "You have to catch the ball in the Super Bowl!"

The Packers had clearly lost their touch. And with the fourth quarter set to start, Pittsburgh had reached the Packers' 33-yard line trailing 21–17.

On the Green Bay sideline, the NFL Films cameras caught a poignant conversation between linebackers coach Kevin Greene and his prized pupil, Clay Matthews. Greene said to Matthews, "Everybody looks up to Wood [Charles Woodson] as being a leader. Well, he's gone. Nobody's standing up and rallying the troops. It is time. It is time."

Remember what McCarthy told his team earlier in the week? "Trust your preparation." Well, the way the Packers stemmed the tide and turned the game around was all about preparation.

Matthews recognized a Steelers formation from his film study the previous two weeks. He anticipated a running play right at him.

On the first play of the quarter, Packers defensive end Ryan Pickett and Matthews combined to blow up Mendenhall. Matthews stood him up on the front side, while Pickett got his helmet on the ball from behind and forced a fumble that linebacker Desmond Bishop recovered.

The Packers had stemmed the momentum. Now, could they turn the tide in Super Bowl XLV?

The Pack Is Back

The Packers hadn't converted a third down since their first touchdown drive of the first quarter and there was no reason to think they were going to convert now. The Pittsburgh defense was in control of the game now.

The Packers faced third-and-7 at their own 48-yard line when Rodgers threw complete to James Jones on a 12-yard sideline route. Finally, a conversion!

Then, after Nelson dropped a crossing route for a certain first down, the Packers faced a third-and-10 from Pittsburgh's 40. The Steelers rushed five, but couldn't get close to Rodgers, in large part because running back Brandon Jackson stoned blitzing cornerback Bryant McFadden in the hole.

Nelson had single coverage and whipped Clark on an inside slant. The terrific blocking up front allowed Rodgers to step into the throw, and he delivered a strike to Nelson that went for 38 yards to Pittsburgh's 2-yard line.

"If you play this game long enough in this position, you are going to drop the ball," Nelson said. "You have to move on. We are levelheaded. We don't get too high and we don't get too low as a whole wide receiver corps.

"We weren't panicking at all when Pittsburgh started coming back. We just said, 'Okay, we have to go make plays.' We knew it was going to be on us and that is why we stepped up and made plays."

Rodgers and Jennings combined to make Green Bay's next big play.

All night long, Jennings had been asking, calling, even pleading for the corner route.

"They can't cover it!" Jennings exclaimed.

Well, Jennings got his wish.

On second-and-goal from Pittsburgh's 8-yard line, Green Bay employed an empty backfield, and after the ball was snapped, Rodgers quickly looked left.

Rodgers had no intention of ever going left, mind you. He was simply trying to get Polamalu—the NFL's Defensive Player of the Year—to drift that way.

It was a continuation of a 60-minute battle that Rodgers waged—and won—with the safety.

"He's a guy that you have to be aware of him, where he's at all times," Rodgers said of Polamalu. "He's a great player, had a great season, but guys have to respect where my eyes are looking so it was important to me to use good eye control on the field and not stare anybody down because he can cover a lot of ground quickly.

"When he was down in the box, we made sure he was picked up in the protection schemes. A couple of times when he came on blitzes, we adjusted the protection to make sure we had him picked up because he's a very talented blitzer and when he's high, a deep safety, you just have to make sure you are good with your eyes."

Rodgers was sublime on this play. Polamalu watched Rodgers' eyes and cheated back to the left, which allowed Jennings to come free in the right corner. Rodgers lofted another perfect ball and Jennings' touchdown grab gave Green Bay a 28–17 lead.

"That was completely my fault," Polamalu said afterward. "Earlier in the game they ran Jennings down the middle and I was anticipating that same pass play, and I guessed wrong."

True to their championship pedigree, Pittsburgh came roaring back with a seven-play, 66-yard drive that took just more than four minutes. The Steelers' scoring strike came when the speedy Wallace got behind Shields, and Roethlisberger put the ball right on his fingertips for a 25-yard touchdown.

Antwaan Randle El scored on an option pitch for the two-point conversion, and the Steelers were within 28–25. There was still 7:34 left in what had become a Super Bowl thriller.

"I thought we were going to win," Wallace said. "We never think we are going to lose. We have no doubt in our mind that we are going to win the game."

Rodgers and the Packers took over on their 25, but after a sack and a false-start penalty on guard Daryn Colledge, they quickly faced a third-and-10. Pittsburgh rushed just three, which meant Rodgers would have to be razor-sharp to beat the eight-man coverage in back.

Jennings, working from the left slot, ran another seam route against Steelers No. 1 cornerback Ike Taylor. The ball was out of Rodgers' hands in 2.8 seconds, and he had perhaps a 12-inch window to squeeze the ball into.

He did. It was arguably the throw of Rodgers' life, one that went for 31 yards and kept the Steelers offense grounded.

"It seemed like it brushed off the tip of Ike Taylor's glove," Jennings said. "But it just got over the top enough where I could make a play on it."

A pair of runs by Starks netted 15 yards. Then Rodgers threw a gorgeous back-shoulder pass to Jones for 21 yards to Pittsburgh's 8-yard line.

On third-and-goal, though, Rodgers' fade for Nelson in the right corner of the end zone missed by inches. Green Bay was forced to settle for a Mason Crosby field goal, and its lead was a precarious 31–25 with 2:07 still remaining.

I said on Packers radio, "The Packers have taken a 31–25 lead, but failed to deliver the dagger."

Rodgers knew it, too.

"I was just disappointed we didn't finish off with seven," Rodgers said. "We talked about it with seven minutes left when we got the ball. 'Hey, let's take it down and score and we're the champs.'

"We made a couple of big plays on third down, but unfortunately, I just missed Jordy on that third down on the goal line. I was just praying our guys would come up with one more stop."

Final Act

One more act remained in Super Bowl XLV. So often in this season and so often in the postseason, it came down to Green Bay's underappreciated defense getting a stop to preserve a win.

Two years earlier, Roethlisberger led the Steelers 78 yards in the closing moments of the 43rd Super Bowl and hit Santonio Holmes with a 6-yard touchdown pass to win the game.

Then in Week 15 2009, Roethlisberger and Wallace hooked up on a 19-yard touchdown on the final play of the game to defeat Green Bay 37–36.

Now, Roethlisberger would get a chance to repeat history.

"We've been doing this all year long," said Williams. "The defense has been put in that situation and that spot all year long and we rose to the challenge each and every time. That's one thing we emphasized all season; that when adversity hits, that's when we want to step up and make plays and we did that all year long."

The Steelers took over at their 13-yard line with 1:59 remaining following an unnecessary roughness penalty on the kickoff.

On first down, Rothlisberger hit tight end Heath Miller for 15 yards and a first down to the 28. The Steelers were out of the hole.

Roethlisberger then connected with veteran receiver Hines Ward for five yards to the 33-yard line and the march was on. The Steelers seemed to have communication issues, though, and Roethlisberger threw consecutive incompletions to Wallace and Ward on balls that weren't even close.

Now it was fourth-and-5, and the 45th Super Bowl came down to one play. For the Packers, it was simple: make a stop and win a title.

"Everybody was just praying," Shields said.

Green Bay rushed five and ran a fire zone in back. Roethlisberger threw to his left for Wallace, but Williams broke on the ball perfectly and knocked it to the ground. The Steelers wanted a pass interference call, but Williams' technique was perfect and no flags were warranted.

Green Bay had held. Only 49 seconds remained.

"It was a great feeling because you knew that you had to go in and keep them from scoring a touchdown in the two-minute drill," Capers said. "A year ago when we played them up there, we had the same situation and they scored on the last play of the game to beat us. So it was a great feeling to see the play get made. That's the best feeling in the world."

There was one better: the kneel down.

With Kuhn and Jackson huddled close, Rodgers took consecutive snaps and dropped to a knee. The Packers were champions again, thanks to a memorable 31–25 victory.

"The Super Bowl was the way our whole season was in one win," linebacker Desmond Bishop said. "Ups, downs, roller-coaster rides, people getting hurt, and a momentum swing, [and] we showed resilience again. We just kept fighting, and stayed as one."

Reflections

In Super Bowl XLV the Packers scored 21 points off three Pittsburgh turnovers. Against the best defense in football, the Packers had no turnovers and captured the fourth Super Bowl in franchise history.

The 2010 Green Bay Packers never trailed in any game by more than seven points. That is an astounding fact! I had never seen a team do that over the course of an entire season, this one lasting 20 games.

I had never seen a club survive so many injuries to make a Super Bowl run. The depth of talent Ted Thompson and his staff built was amazing. But the determination of those players through the adversity and the machinations of their head coach were tantamount to success that year.

"The character in that locker room is like nothing I've ever been a part of," Rodgers said. "It's just a special group of guys who believe in each other and love each other. When someone goes down, somebody steps up and picks each other up."

How strong was the resolve of the 2010 Packers? They faced—and won—six consecutive elimination games.

I will never forget the precision of Aaron Rodgers in that Super Bowl. He won the game of inches time and time again and was now completely out of the shadow of Brett Favre. The team and Packers Nation were his.

"He played great," McCarthy said of Rodgers. "We put everything on his shoulders. He did a lot at the line of scrimmage for us against a great defense. He did a hell of a job."

I will never forget the star-crossed leaders of that team. I felt both good and a little bit sad for Woodson and Driver. They got their Super Bowls, but weren't able to be on the field in the second half due to their injuries.

For all the focus on Green Bay's offense, Dom Capers' defense was championship caliber that season. And the Packers were nowhere near "super" without their defense getting clutch stop after clutch stop near the end of games.

Finally, championship teams today are not "super" at the outset of a season. They evolve to greatness through the season.

In some ways the 2010 Packers were typical of today's "super" teams. Even though they were one of the preseason favorites to win a championship, their string of injuries forced them to evolve into champions.

"We just continued to get better all season," Woodson said. "We continued to fight no matter what adversity we went through. I think late in the season, down the stretch, we just had fun, and today was no different. World champs."

Heading Home

The next day my family dropped me off at the team hotel to catch the bus for the airport and the team charter home to Green Bay.

I remember sitting in the dining room as players were coming and going having breakfast. But I'll never forget seeing Woodson with his arm in a sling and Driver on crutches. Then they pushed Jordy Nelson into the room in a wheelchair. His knee was the size of a pumpkin.

I looked around and marveled, "These guys actually won the game. I wonder what the other guys look like."

On the plane ride home, I saw equipment manager Red Batty

Each member of the Packers' traveling party got a moment with the Lombardi Trophy including play-by-play man and author Wayne Larrivee. (Jim Biever Photography)

polishing the Lombardi Trophy. I didn't think much of it, but he was probably trying to get all the fingerprints off before we got to Green Bay.

Then Batty and team photographer Jim Biever brought the trophy around the plane and each member of the traveling party got to hold it and have his or her picture taken with it. It was a classy gesture by two of the nicest people I have met in sports.

The Lombardi Trophy was heading home. And in the words of the late, great Jim Irwin, the legendary voice of the Packers, it was "where it belongs."

CHAPTER 13
2014, 2015, AND BEYOND

I have a theory about teams in the National Football League today. They evolve as the season progresses. Coach Mike McCarthy would say it's "the process."

I believe if you are "super" in September and October, you won't be by January. The Green Bay Packers' 2014 season mirrored that theory.

The season began where it would eventually end: Seattle. But in between there was a whole lot of growing, because the Packers were by no means "super" coming out of training camp.

Playing the defending Super Bowl Champions on the road to start a season is one of the toughest assignments an NFL season can present. But that was what the Packers faced in their 2014 opener.

Green Bay traveled to Seattle for a nationally televised Thursday-night game. It was also the first game of the 2014 NFL season.

After taking a 7–3 lead in the first quarter, the Packers were outscored 33–9 the rest of the way and lost 36–16. Seattle rushed for 207 yards and its defense held Green Bay to 255 yards of offense in a dominant win.

"Congratulations to Seattle," McCarthy said afterward. "I thought they played very well, really, in a nutshell. [We] definitely did not stop the run. So our fundamental inconsistencies throughout the game coincides with untimely penalties.

"We felt all week coming in here, playing in this environment, against an excellent football team—we had games of momentum swings. And we had to swing it back. And we were not able to do that tonight. So, hard loss, hard defeat."

There was so much talk after the game about the Packers not challenging Seattle's All-Pro cornerback Richard Sherman in the game, but that was just talk-show fodder. My impression was the Packers weren't ready for a game of that magnitude and it had nothing to do with coaching or player preparation. Green Bay simply had not evolved at that early stage of the season. While the Packers may not have been ready for the Seahawks on September 4, by January 18 they'd be more than ready.

The following week, in the home opener at Lambeau Field, it looked like the Packers might not be ready for a bad New York Jets team either. Green Bay trailed 21–3 early in the second quarter.

From there, the defense stiffened, holding the visitors to three points the rest of the day. Rodgers passed for 346 yards and three touchdowns as the Packers rallied for a 31–24 win.

"It's a big difference," Packers defensive end Datone Jones said of being 1–1 instead of 0–2. "You have to win at home, that's the key.

"You have to win at home and should win every game there. Playing at home, you have to win here. It helps you down the road. I'm very excited about what happened today. It wasn't pretty to start, but it's not how you start; it's how you finish. Our defense is a finishing defense."

At Detroit the following week, the offense sputtered again in an ugly 19–7 loss to the Lions. Rodgers threw for just 162 yards and led just one scoring drive. At 1–2, the Packers headed to Chicago with serious questions swirling about what kind of team they were and what kind of team they might become.

That week, on his radio show, Rodgers spelled the word "R-E-L-A-X." Rodgers told the fan base—and more importantly, his team—to relax. He could not have been more prophetic.

The Packers absorbed a 496-yard onslaught by the Chicago offense. But at the end of the day, the Bears managed only 17 points.

Rodgers completed 22-of-28 passes for 302 yards and threw four touchdowns in leading Green Bay to a critical 38–17 win over Chicago. Rodgers' final passer rating of 151.2 was the fourth-highest in franchise history, and he averaged a remarkable 10.79 passing yards per attempt.

"I just know it's a long season," Rodgers said. "There's always going to be mini-freakouts along the way.

"Just have to stick together and stay the course. I just wanted to remind everyone that it's a long season and at some point we are going to get this thing figured out."

Facing the possibility of a two-game losing streak, Rodgers and the offense didn't punt a single time. In the process, Rodgers and the Packers won for the fifth straight time in Chicago. Rodgers also improved his career record against the Bears to 11–3.

Relax? You bet.

"Everyone's going to have rough games, so to speak," Packers right tackle Bryan Bulaga said of Rodgers. "But I know he's competitive as hell and we were just having fun out there today. That's really what it was, having fun, moving the ball.

"That's normally how Aaron plays football. The offense was just working today. We had everything going."

The Packers were 2–2 and had found their offense.

Green Bay won its next three games, including blowout wins over Minnesota and Carolina. In between was a dramatic 27–24 comeback win at Miami.

On a hot and humid 85-degree day, Rodgers led a stirring 11-play, 60-yard drive in the final minute of the game. He hit tight end Andrew Quarless with a four-yard touchdown pass for the dagger.

The Packers had now won four in a row and the offense was rolling, but the defense was still a question. A midseason trip to New Orleans for a nationally televised Sunday-night game would lead to even more questions about the defense.

The Packers allowed 495 total yards, failed to force a single punt, and were routed by the Saints 44–23. Green Bay also didn't force a turnover until the final minute, after both teams had emptied their benches.

"We need to be better than that," McCarthy said. "We need to be a football team that does more than rely on winning the turnover ratio to win."

The midpoint of the season had arrived. And while the Packers were a respectable 5–3, their defense appeared to be in trouble.

Green Bay's switch that offseason to a smaller, quicker defensive front had been completely ineffective against the run. Adding to the problem was the Packers' inside linebacker play had been subpar.

At the midway point of the season, the Packers ranked dead last in rushing yards allowed per game at 153.5 and were 28th in yards allowed per carry (4.8). In 2013, Green Bay finished 25th in rushing yards allowed per game (125.0) and 29th in yards allowed per carry (4.6).

Saints running back Mark Ingram entered Week 8 with 159 rushing yards on the season. Then Ingram hammered the Packers with 172 rushing yards and averaged 7.2 yards per carry.

Prior to that contest, Ingram had one 100-yard game in 40 career contests.

"We were clicking," Ingram said afterward. "The offensive line, it started with them. They did a great job of getting push off the ball and creating seams for me to run through and just be able to run hard. All credit to the O-line because without them, nights like this aren't possible."

During the bye week that followed, Packers defensive coordinator Dom Capers made the bold, unorthodox move of moving his best player—Clay Matthews—from outside linebacker to inside linebacker.

"Over the bye week, it's like anything," Packers head coach Mike McCarthy said. "You have a chance to kind of reboot, reset yourself for the second half of the season.

"Playing Clay in different areas, this year the different position to create targeting problems for the offense was something that we spent the whole offseason highlighting and this was kind of the next step. Great job by our defensive staff with the creativity."

Taking Matthews off the edge, where he was one of the league's best pass rushers, and moving him inside could have potentially weakened two positions. But the Packers were desperate, and Matthews isn't just any player. His athleticism, energy, and savvy injected into the middle of the Packers' defense turned out to be just what the doctor ordered.

In Green Bay's first game after the bye, Matthews gave a rousing performance that included 11 tackles, two tackles for loss and one sack. With Matthews leading the way, Green Bay's defense gave a spirited performance in its 55–14 rout of visiting Chicago.

With Matthews extremely active, instinctive, and at times unblockable, Green Bay limited Chicago to just 55 rushing yards, the fewest allowed by the Packers since Baltimore gained only 47 in Week 6 of 2013. The Bears also averaged just 2.3 yards per carry, a far cry from the late-September game when Chicago ran for 235 yards and averaged 4.7 yards per rush.

"I mean I was in great position to make a lot of plays tonight and I think that's ultimately the reason why we needed to make a few changes around here," Matthews said. "I've always taken pride in whatever they've asked me to do, so you put me in position where there's some free space and some opportunities to make some plays, I took advantage of it. So, I think this is what we wanted out of this change and we'll see what that means going forward."

The only one to overshadow Matthews that night might have been Rodgers. Rodgers had a night for the ages, joining Oakland's Daryle Lamonica as the only players in NFL history to throw six first-half touchdown passes.

Rodgers needed just seven possessions—and 36 offensive plays—to notch his accomplishment and power the Packers to a remarkably easy win. Rodgers went 18-of-24 in the first half alone with six touchdown strikes, 315 passing yards, and a nearly perfect passer rating of 156.3.

Little-used tight end Brandon Bostick caught the first touchdown, and tight end Andrew Quarless hauled in No. 2. Jordy Nelson continued his Pro Bowl season with scoring strikes of 73 and 40 yards. And after Eddie Lacy had a brilliant 56-yard catch-and-run for a score, Randall Cobb had a one-handed, diving 18-yard touchdown reception.

By halftime, the Packers led 42–0. The NFL's oldest rivalry had turned into a laughingstock.

"I can promise you this is not easy," Rodgers said. "It's not easy to do this every week. We put a lot of time in—we all do—and we prepare to be successful.

"There's a high expectation on our plays based on the number of checks that we do and the game plan every week to have creative input, but to also make the game plan work. It's tough to go out and execute like that, but that's what happens when everybody kind of works together and believes in each other."

The Packers made it back-to-back 50-point games when they ripped apart the Philadelphia Eagles 53–20 the following week. Green Bay held the NFC's highest-scoring team 11 points below its average. The offense also left no doubt, rolling to a 30–6 lead by halftime.

Ageless outside linebacker Julius Peppers put an exclamation point on the scoring by returning an interception 52 yards for a touchdown in the third quarter.

The Packers improved to a perfect 5–0 at home and had outscored their foes 219–85 in those games. Green Bay's margin of victory in home games was 26.8 points—a mark unseen since the days the Packers were playing the Marinette Northerners and the Oshkosh Professionals more than 90 years ago.

The Packers, who had posted 55 points against visiting Chicago seven days earlier, registered 50-plus points for the second straight game. That marked the first time in franchise history that Green Bay scored 50 points in consecutive games and just the fifth time in NFL history that a team accomplished the feat.

"We have a great home-field advantage, probably the best in football, and it's a special place to play," Packers coach Mike McCarthy said. "Obviously we enjoy playing here. This is our element. This is where we live. This is where we train. So we're obviously comfortable."

Philadelphia came to Green Bay with a 7–2 record, leading the NFC East and in the fight for a lofty playoff seed. But the Eagles were dealt their worst defeat in 26 games.

"This has all been unfolding like we want it to," cornerback Tramon Williams said. "We've done a good job stopping the run, getting in favorable down and distances and the offense is scoring points. If offense scores points like that and we can play good solid defense like that the whole time, this could be something special.

"Right now, I'd say it's going to be tough for someone to beat us here. We haven't played like this, ever. We've played well, but not like this. If we are playing like this at home, then obviously people probably won't want to come here. It's not going to easy at all, but it's pretty great how we're playing right now."

The following week, Green Bay edged Minnesota 24–21 on a cold day at TCF Bank Stadium on the campus of the University of Minnesota. Eddie Lacy and the ground game came to the forefront in this one.

Lacy rushed for 125 yards and the Packers posted 155 rushing yards to extend their latest winning streak to three games. With identical 8–3 records, the Packers and Lions were waging a two-team battle for the NFC North Division title.

As this 2014 season went along, you could see different elements of the Packers' game come together almost week-to-week. First, they got the passing game on track in Week 4 at Chicago. The run defense was adjusted during the bye week, and in the second half of the season, the Packers held four of eight opponents under 100 yards rushing and no team ran for more than 113 yards.

Then, right on cue, Eddie Lacy and Green Bay's running game came up big. In the first half of the season, the Packers rushed for 100 yards just three times. In the second half of the campaign they rushed for 100-plus yards in every game.

Over the final eight games of the regular season, the Packers averaged

142.1 rushing yards per game. Green Bay also averaged 4.7 yards per carry and ran the ball 30.1 times per game.

The offense was complete, a threat both through the air and on the ground. The defense was containing the run, but the biggest test of the season was next to come.

The New England Patriots and the Green Bay Packers were experiencing somewhat similar seasons by late November. Like the Packers, the Patriots started the season 2–2 after falling at Kansas City 41–14 in Week 4. Everyone was writing New England off, just as they had done with the Packers following their 1–2 start.

Both quarterbacks—New England's Tom Brady and Green Bay's Rodgers—were playing at a remarkably high level, too.

Brady overcame a rough start to the season and had led the Patriots to seven straight wins and a 9–2 record that was tied for the best mark in football. Brady had thrown 26 touchdown passes to just six interceptions, and he had a passer rating of 101.0.

Rodgers had won NFL MVP honors in 2011 when he set a new league mark for quarterback passer rating in a season (122.5).

Believe it or, Rodgers had been even better in 2014.

Rodgers entered the New England game with 30 touchdown passes and just three interceptions. That ratio of 10-to-1 not only led the NFL, it was better than the remarkable 8.5-to-1 mark Rodgers had in 2011 (45 TDs, 6 INTs).

Rodgers had an NFL-best passer rating of 119.2. And Rodgers had led the Packers to wins in seven of their last eight games, an 8–3 overall mark, and the No. 2 seed in the NFC if the postseason had started then.

"Aaron's been playing just off the charts," Packers safety Morgan Burnett said. "We see it every day in practice. I'm just glad he's on our team and we don't have to go against him in a game.

"Tom [Brady], he's unbelievable too. He's been great for a long time. They're both fantastic players."

The matchup between the Patriots and Packers was considered to be a Super Bowl preview by many. The morning of the game, I encountered Patriots coach Bill Belichick on the field showing some scraggly-haired kid around Lambeau Field like a tourist. The scraggly-haired kid was apparently his son.

Say what you will about Belichick, but he has a deep appreciation for the history of the game, and there is no more historic place in the NFL today than Lambeau Field. The most successful coach of this era was taking it all in. It was like he was doing his bucket-list trip to Lambeau.

As Belichick approached, I said, "Hi, Coach." He grumbled some gruff, inaudible response, giving me the pleasure of being "dissed" by the great Belichick. It was the start of a great football day and evening in Green Bay!

People ask me all the time, "How are the Packers going to do this week?" When it comes to the Packers and my preparation each week, I am one of those people who is too close to the forest to see the trees.

When my kids have a little doubt about how the Packers might play in a given week, they ask me for my objective opinion. When I tell them, of course off the record, I think the Packers are going to struggle this week, they take delight. That's because nine out of 10 times, I am completely wrong. Oh, and by the way, no one is happier than me to be wrong when the Packers end up winning the game.

After preparing all week for the game, I didn't see how the Packers were going to beat this New England team, which was at the top of its game. What happened next was, once again, a pleasant surprise—at least to me.

New England at Green Bay might have been the best overall football game of the entire 2014 NFL regular season. Both sides brought their "A" game to historic Lambeau Field.

The Patriots had arguably the best starting tandem of cornerbacks in the league with Darrelle Revis and Brandon Browner. But Rodgers took advantage of the drop off to No. 3 corner Kyle Arrington and dime back Logan Ryan.

Rookie wide receiver Davante Adams, the Packers' No. 3 wide receiver, was targeted seven times in the first half. Adams caught three passes for 90 yards, but also dropped a touchdown pass.

The Packers took the opening drive 58 yards to a field goal. They later drove 66 yards in 11 plays to another field goal. That was my only concern—that the Packers were settling for field goals instead of finishing drives in the red zone. I worried it was just a matter of time before those truncated drives would come back to haunt the Packers.

Two Mason Crosby field goals and a 32-yard touchdown pass from Aaron Rodgers to Richard Rodgers staked the Packers to a 13–0 lead at the end of the first quarter.

New England responded with a five-play, 73-yard drive. Patriots' running back Brandon Bolden scored on a six-yard run to start the second quarter. Crosby answered with another field goal—then Brady drove the visitors 80 yards in 12 plays and hit Brandon LaFell on a two-yard touchdown pass, cutting the deficit to 16–14.

In the final minute of the half, though, the Packers countered with an electric five-play, 81-yard drive. Rodgers hooked up with Nelson on a 45-yard touchdown strike and beat the great Darrelle Revis to put the Packers on top 23–14 at the half.

"That was big," Rodgers said of the touchdown just before halftime. "We decided to scat Eddie [Lacy] out and have a combination we like, Jordy run an in breaker, put the ball slightly behind him. He made a great catch and he's been great in the open field. Just an incredibly athletic play there at the goal line."

Following a scoreless third quarter, New England cut the gap to 23–21 on another Brady-to-LaFell touchdown pass just one minute into the fourth quarter. Crosby banged home another field goal to give Green Bay a 26–21 lead with 8:45 left, setting up a dramatic ending.

Going into that fourth-quarter drive, Brady had directed 35 game-winning drives in the fourth quarter or overtime in the regular season in his illustrious career. In the fourth quarter at Lambeau Field, in a one-possession game, he was at it again.

Brady and the Patriots took over at the New England 28-yard line with 8:41 remaining. Brady did what Brady does: he drove his team 52 yards in 11 plays to the Green Bay 20-yard line. The Patriots were driving, they had momentum and there was no doubt what was going to happen next. We've seen this way too many times, right?

This is where I first saw "super" in the Packers that season. On third-and-9, Mike Daniels and Mike Neal sacked Brady, the only time he went down all day, for a loss of nine. That forced a 47-yard field goal attempt by Steven Gostkowski, and he pushed it wide right. Like in the "Super Season" of 2010, it was the defense that stood up!

"They're really, really good," Neal said of the Patriots. "They're methodical, systematic, and they just don't make mistakes.

"We just knew we had to adjust to the game and once we adjusted to the game we could stop them. And once we did that, we just cashed in on the plays we needed to."

Right or wrong, I'm still a little old school. I believe defense still wins championships. The 2011 Packers had the greatest offense in the history of the franchise. But that team didn't win a playoff game.

Why? Because those Packers did not have a defense that could do what the 2014 defense did against the Patriots—make a stop with the game on the line. Maybe this Packers team was evolving into something special.

The Packers took over with 2:40 to go in the game and quickly bled the final timeouts from Belichick and the Patriots. Then on third-and-4, Rodgers threw the dagger—a tracer over the middle into coverage. Randall Cobb made the catch for a seven-yard gain and a first down to essentially end the contest.

"Excellent Lambeau Field win," McCarthy said. "I thought the crowd was phenomenal. Excellent football team in the New England Patriots, with the big challenge that they bring to the table. I thought offensively we had a lot of productivity. The point total was enough to win the game. I thought the defense did a lot of good things, and really I think the end of the game is what you're looking for as a coach.

"Each unit—the offense, the defense, the special teams—you need to make key plays down the stretch and we accomplished that tonight. There was really good things situationally, I thought they challenged us throughout the game with a number of adjustments. I thought our players handled our adjustments very well. So excellent win for us."

What a game it was! Both teams played well. But I thought the Packers had a discernible advantage at one position—quarterback.

The difference between future Hall of Famer Tom Brady in his late 30s and Aaron Rodgers was the latter had mobility that the veteran Brady no longer possessed. Time and again, Rodgers bought time with his legs. His athleticism at that position was big on that day. If this was a Super Bowl preview, well then, the Super Bowl was truly going to be super!

"This was awesome," defensive end Mike Daniels said. "I mean, that's a Hall of Fame quarterback right there. His tight end [Rob Gronkowski] is the like the Terminator. They've got a running back [LeGarrette Blount] that's my size with a very experienced offensive line. And some receivers that run all over the place, so that's a dangerous team. We came out with a win today. The offensive guys did a heck of a job and we just did what we had to do on our side of the ball to ensure the win."

Green Bay defeated Atlanta 43–37 on *Monday Night Football* and improved to 10–3. The Packers then took a five-game winning streak into Buffalo on a grey, cool day.

Green Bay entered that game leading the league in scoring and ranked sixth in passing yards. Rodgers was also the top-rated quarterback in the league.

That's why few could have predicted what happened that day.

The Packers' offense played one of their worst games ever under the McCarthy–Rodgers leadership. Rodgers threw two interceptions, the Packers converted just 29 percent of their third downs, and Green Bay's receivers dropped five passes.

Nelson dropped what would have been a 94-yard touchdown pass that could have changed the complexion of the game in the third quarter.

"We had exactly what we wanted," Nelson said. "We just didn't make the play. I short-armed it and dropped it."

I have never seen Rodgers struggle like he did that day, when he completed just 17-of-42 passes for 185 yards, no touchdowns, two interceptions, and a passer rating of 34.3. That was Rodgers' worst passer rating as a starting quarterback.

"It was frustrating," Rodgers said. "Some days are going to be like this. We set the standard pretty high, and we like to live up to it every week."

Overall, the Packers picked a bad day to have their poorest offensive showing of the season, because their defense played well in what became a 21–13 loss. Little did we know at the time, that game in Orchard Park, New York, would have a profound impact on a much bigger game in January.

Green Bay got back on track with a 20–3 victory at Tampa the following week. In that game, though, Rodgers suffered a calf injury that would impact his mobility the rest of the season.

Next up were the red-hot Detroit Lions, who were on a roll with four straight wins. Both teams entered the regular season finale with 11–4 records in a winner-take-all NFC North championship game.

This was old hat for the Packers, who were trying for their third straight division title. It was the same situation they had faced the season before in Chicago, when Rodgers and Cobb hooked up for a memorable last-minute touchdown that gave the Packers a 33–28 win and the NFC North Championship.

One year later, a division title, a bye week, and a home divisional playoff game were at stake.

With Rodgers limited by his calf injury, McCarthy put in a pistol formation that would reduce the footwork required of the quarterback. This is a formation where the quarterback is three or four yards behind center with the running back lined up directly behind him. You could put setbacks to the left and right of the quarterback in a "fully loaded pistol." Or you could just add a fullback or tight end to one side of the quarterback for a "half-loaded pistol."

Much would depend on the protection they were looking for on a given play. Sometimes one of those "up" backs would go in motion, giving the defense a different look. More than anything, the formation limited the amount of footwork required by the quarterback to execute either a handoff to the running back or reduce the amount of back-steps required to get normal depth for a pass play. There was no pulling back from center nor a great deal of lateral movement required by the quarterback.

Rodgers was working behind the best Green Bay offensive line since the great unit that paved the way for Ahman Green in the early 2000s. From left to right were David Bakhtiari, Josh Sitton, Corey Linsley, T.J. Lang, and Bryan Bulaga. The group was arguably the second-best line in football that year, ranking only behind a sensational group in Dallas.

In my opinion, though, Green Bay's group was the best pass-blocking line in football. Now, with their field general robbed of one of his greatest weapons, his mobility, they would have to protect like never before.

The Packers ran the ball six times on their opening drive before passing it. In the entire first half, Rodgers attempted just nine passes. On their 26 offensive snaps, the Packers ran 17 times.

However, Rodgers left the game late in the second quarter, sending Packer Nation into a panic. The Packers led 7–0 when Rodgers rolled to his right and flipped a four-yard touchdown pass to Cobb. Just as he was delivering the ball, though, Rodgers collapsed as if he'd been shot in the back of the leg.

Rodgers had to be helped off the field, then was carted back to the Packers' locker room.

"Just moved out of the pocket there, felt a very similar feeling in a different spot as I did last week," Rodgers said. "I was worried about the severity of the injury and my ability to walk off the field at that point. But once I got back in the locker room I was actually watching the game on TV with some heat on my calf thinking if I could finagle myself to go back in."

He did.

Rodgers and Dr. Pat McKenzie, Green Bay's team physician, had a long discussion at halftime. And McKenzie agreed to let Rodgers test out the calf.

Rodgers got re-taped and also kept heat on the injury. Still, No. 2 quarterback Matt Flynn led the opening drive of the second half.

Shortly thereafter, Rodgers came out of the tunnel to a crowd giddy to see him return. There was just one problem. In the eight minutes of football time Rodgers missed, the Lions had stormed back and tied the game 14–14.

Rodgers threw a few passes on the sideline, and also dropped and planted. And when McKenzie approved, it was all systems go.

"Just felt like if I could get back in there it might give us a little jolt, and wanted to be out there with the guys competing," Rodgers said.

Rodgers did more than that. With the division title—and a first-round playoff bye—on the line, he played terrific football again.

On Rodgers' first series back, he hit Cobb for 29 yards on a crossing route to the Lions' 19-yard line. Three plays later, Cobb whipped Detroit nickel cornerback Cassius Vaughn and Rodgers hit him for an 18-yard touchdown.

Two series later, Rodgers drove Green Bay to the Lions' 1-yard line. On second-and-1, Rodgers called his own number, then fell forward for an awkward one-yard touchdown that gave Green Bay a 28–14 lead.

The Packers went on to a 30–20 win, clinched the No. 2 seed in the postseason, and earned a much-needed first-round bye.

Afterward, some players compared this to Michael Jordan playing with the flu and leading Chicago to the 1997 NBA title. Others brought up the name Willis Reed, referring to the New York Knicks center's heroic effort in Game 7 of the 1970 NBA Finals.

"When I step back and think about this season and this game years from now, I'll probably take a lot of pride in getting back out there and letting my teammates know I'll put my body on the line for them," Rodgers said. "We're in the moment. It's about winning the division and getting a home playoff game.

"You're just out there competing. This is what we love to do. I'm passionate about this game. I love the competition, and I love being out there with my guys and having them count on me to be myself. This is a good night and good things to come."

The Packers certainly needed the time off that a bye week afforded. Their quarterback was a little more mobile when Dallas came to Green Bay for the divisional playoff game two weeks later. It was the first postseason trip to Green Bay for the Cowboys since the Ice Bowl on December 31, 1967.

Dallas led 14–10 at halftime, but Green Bay countered with a field goal. Then, Dallas running back DeMarco Murray—the NFL's leading rusher scored on a one-yard touchdown run, capping an 80-yard drive that gave Dallas a 21–13 advantage with 4:12 to go in the third quarter.

Murray pounded the Green Bay run defense to the tune of 123 rushing yards on 25 carries that day. That 21–13 score could have been even worse had Packers outside linebacker Julius Peppers not made a sensational play, stripping Murray of the football on a third-quarter run. The fumble was recovered by Packers defensive end Datone Jones and led to a Crosby field goal. On that play, Murray had an open field to the end zone on what might have been a 59-yard touchdown gallop.

The murmur of the crowd, the body language of the players—this had all the markings of another postseason letdown at home for Green Bay. I kept flashing back to Michael Vick and the Falcons drubbing the Packers 27–7 to end the 2002 campaign at Lambeau Field. That was the first postseason loss at home in the history of the Green Bay franchise.

There was the 31–17 nightmare loss to the Vikings in the 2004 postseason when Randy Moss mooned the south end zone stands. The Packers fell in overtime 23–20 to the New York Giants in the 2007 NFC Championship Game, then lost to those same Giants 37–20 in the 2011 NFC divisional playoffs. Finally, in 2013, the Packers suffered a 23–20 loss to the San Francisco 49ers in a wild-card game.

Five times in 11 years, the Packers suffered a home playoff loss. Five times.

Then Rodgers did what great players do. He got hot at just the right moment.

With the Packers in a 21–13 hole late in the third quarter, McCarthy changed his approach. Instead of max protecting and leaning on the run game, McCarthy and Rodgers opened up the offense.

The Packers spread the Cowboys out with four- and five-receiver looks and let Rodgers go to work.

First, Rodgers engineered a seven-play, 90-yard touchdown march that pulled the Packers within one at 21–20. Rodgers hit Randall Cobb for 26 yards, then fired a 46-yard touchdown to Davante Adams on third-and-15, as the rookie wideout beat Sterling Moore and J.J. Wilcox for the score.

"Just because I may have had a drop or two in previous weeks, his confidence in me is the same as my confidence in him," Adams said of his connection with Rodgers. "We've done a lot since I've been here. I've caught a lot more than I've dropped so the fact that he stays in there with me means a lot to me. So I've just got to just make sure I keep doing what I've got to do."

One series later, Rodgers led an eight-play, 80-yard scoring drive in which 78 of the yards came via Rodgers' right arm.

The drive included an 18-yard pass to Adams, a 14-yarder to Cobb, and a 13-yard strike to tight end Andrew Quarless. Rodgers capped the march with a 13-yard bullet touchdown to Richard Rodgers that gave Green Bay a lead it wouldn't relinquish.

"The guys did a good job getting open," Aaron Rodgers said. "The line gave me a lot of time and I expect to be accurate. I was able to throw some balls on rhythm and put them where I wanted."

Rodgers injured his calf in two spots over the final two games of the regular season, then didn't practice for 11 days. But after a slow start against Dallas, Rodgers heated up as the game went along.

Rodgers connected on his final 10 passes. And in the second half alone, Rodgers completed 15-of-20 passes for 226 yards and two touchdowns, and posted a passer rating of 145.0.

"Just an incredible game for Aaron and I think especially for what he's been through the last two weeks," Packers coach Mike McCarthy said.

There was still a long ways to go, though. Dallas took over at its 18-yard line with 9:10 remaining in the game and Murray ripped off a 30-yard run to start the drive.

Quarterback Tony Romo drove the Cowboys to the Packers' 32-yard line, where on fourth-and-2 he went for it all. Dallas Pro Bowl wide receiver Dez Bryant leaped high in the air, adjusted to the ball, and Green Bay cornerback Sam Shields was unable to make a play on the pass.

Bryant came tumbling down inside the Packers' 1-yard line following a spectacular catch. However, someone in the Green Bay coaching box saw something.

Someone saw the ball come loose before Bryant made what's deemed a "football move." The Packers challenged, and eventually the ruling on the field of a catch was reversed.

"Well I do think he made [the catch], yes, yes, and we had the opportunity to look at several [camera] angles up there where we were sitting from replay and the answer is I do," Cowboys owner Jerry Jones said. "I'm not so much into talking about the judgment of the officials as I am it was just a bad time for us to have a play like that.

"To Green Bay's credit, they were in a position to win the game and they had to make a play like that. It's a shame because we had a great year and I know how much our fans appreciate the work we've done."

It was a classic modern-day "was it a catch?" or "wasn't it a catch?" play—the kind of play that fans everywhere find so maddening. But eruption of the fans at Lambeau Field when referee Tony Corrente announced the reversal was deafening!

"The roar of the Lambeau crowd reminded me of the way they reacted during the 1989 "Instant Replay" game against Chicago. Upon further review that day, the officials ruled that Packers quarterback Don Majkowski did not cross the line of scrimmage when he connected with Sterling Sharpe on a game-winning touchdown pass."

"I've never seen that a day in my life," Bryant said. "I'm just trying to wait and see. I want to know why it wasn't a catch."

The Packers took over at their own 33-yard line with 4:06 to go. The Dallas defense was beaten and battered. They hadn't stopped the Packers since the opening drive of the second half. They weren't going to stop the Packers from sealing the deal either.

Green Bay drove 39 yards in seven plays to the Dallas 28-yard line, before Rodgers employed the victory formation, knelt down three times, and killed the clock.

Green Bay had survived and advanced after a 26–21 decision.

"A great playoff victory," McCarthy said. "The game had everything I am sure you want to see in a football game. We knew it was going to be a big challenge here today and that's exactly what it was."

I have been asked many times—What if the replay upheld the call on the field that Bryant caught the ball at the Green Bay 1-yard line? What if the Cowboys scored on that drive to take the lead?

In my opinion, there is no reason to think the Packers wouldn't have come right back down field and driven for a winning score against that tired Cowboys defense. The Packers almost scored trying to kill the clock on that last drive. That was a defensive unit that gave up 425 yards of offense that day. If Bryant's catch had been upheld and the Cowboys took the lead, the Packers would have still won the game. It just would have been more dramatic.

The Packers were in their third NFC Championship Game in the last eight years, but they would be on the road at Seattle, where the 2014 season began.

The Packers and Seahawks both finished the regular season with 12–4 records. The title game was in Seattle, though, because the Seahawks had won their head-to-head matchup with Green Bay back in Week 1.

The only reason there was a tiebreaker involved was Green Bay's loss at Buffalo on that grey afternoon in mid-December. When you look back, had the Packers not had "one of those days" and taken care of business, they would have finished 13–3 and hosted the NFC Championship game at Lambeau Field.

Now they were returning to Seattle, where the defending World Champion Seahawks had beaten them 36–16 just four-and-a-half months earlier.

"It's going to be a tough game," Packers right guard T.J. Lang said. "Going up to Seattle, you know it's going to be loud, you know they're going to play just fast and physical and we have got to be prepared for it. But we like the way we're playing too. Grinded out some wins here lately.

"It's going to be a good matchup, so we're excited about going back out there and, like I said, we're a lot different team than the first week we went out there. We tried to form an identity. We still didn't know what we had yet, but I think we know what we have now. We like what we have so it's going to be a great matchup. It's going to be a tough one, we understand that, but we'll be ready for the challenge."

It was hard for me to get a feel for this game. The Packers were playing well, but so was Seattle.

Both clubs had survived early-season missteps to win their divisions and prevail in hard-fought divisional playoff games. Seattle beat Carolina 31–17 in the divisional playoffs and had won nine of its last 10 games, including seven in a row.

The Seahawks were 25–2 at home since the start of the 2012 season with an average margin of victory of 14.3 points. CenturyLink Field is widely regarded as the NFL's loudest venue, making it an incredible challenge for opposing offenses.

Seattle's defense was arguably the league's finest since the great Chicago Bears units in the mid-1980s. On the flip side, Green Bay finished with the NFL's No. 1 scoring offense.

On paper, this was strength vs. strength. The defending Super Bowl–champion Seahawks opened as 7.5-point favorites.

"I think this team likes being an underdog," Packers rookie center Corey Linsley said. "No one thought we were going to beat New England. Some people didn't think we'd beat Detroit. So that's all fine with us."

There was a quiet confidence about the Packers that week as they prepared for the daunting task of unseating the champs on their home turf. We went to the game on a Friday night instead of the usual Saturday departure. McCarthy wanted his team to get a workout in Seattle and be adjusted to the time change. The players couldn't wait to get there!

The day before the game one of the assistant coaches came up to me and incredulously asked, "Wayne, why doesn't anyone outside of our group think we can win this game?" Clearly the Packers thought they could win. In fact, they were counting on it!

"First off, you don't get a lot of second chances against those guys, so

I like that," Packers tight end Andrew Quarless said. "That puts a little chip in your shoulder.

"Also, I don't think that first game was completely terrible. We just made some mistakes. We know what we have to do. It should be good. I look forward to it and definitely think it will be a different game."

Green Bay's defense had improved significantly in the second half of the season, and knowing what the offense was capable of, there was certainly reason for confidence in the Packers' camp. I knew how much Green Bay had improved over the course of the season. I just didn't know if they were ready to knock off Seattle in Seattle.

The game these clubs played in September was relatively irrelevant, because both squads had evolved since then. During the second half of the season, the Seahawks had transitioned from an offense keyed by All-Pro running back Marshawn Lynch to one led by quarterback Russell Wilson, who was fast becoming a clutch playmaker.

Wilson won games with his arm, his feet, and most of all his intellect. In 2014, Wilson rushed for 849 yards, the fifth-most by a quarterback in NFL history.

"Russell will do his thing, but they've got a lot of hungry young guys catching the ball that maybe weren't drafted high," Williams said. "But they work hard, buy into things, and in the process become darn good players. Then Russell can make some guys better."

By championship weekend, I saw just three "super" teams—the New England Patriots in the AFC and Green Bay and Seattle in the NFC. The Patriots hammered Indianapolis 45–7 in the AFC Championship game, which would come to be known for Deflategate after the Packers and Seahawks played a legendary game for the NFC Title.

A mid-January Sunday morning in Seattle was predictably rainy. In fact, before the game it rained in monsoon proportions. But the moisture subsided and the Packers and Seahawks kicked off at 12:06 PM Pacific Standard Time.

The Packers took the opening kickoff and drove smartly to the Seattle 29-yard line, where Rodgers went deep into the right side of the end zone only to be picked off by All-Pro cornerback Richard Sherman.

Seattle's first drive ended in an interception as well. Packers rookie safety Ha Ha Clinton-Dix intercepted Wilson's pass to Jermaine Kearse at the Seattle 30-yard line. But a taunting penalty by Packers defensive lineman Mike Daniels cost Green Bay 15 yards.

From there the Packers drove to the Seattle 1-yard line, where they settled for a field goal and a 3–0 lead.

On the ensuing kickoff Brad Jones forced a fumble by Doug Baldwin, and Green Bay safety Morgan Burnett recovered at the Seattle 23-yard line. The Packers had a chance to take a double-digit lead in the game, but the Seahawks again stiffened at the 1-yard line and Crosby made another chip-shot field goal to give Green Bay a 6–0 advantage.

Afterward, Rodgers said he would have liked the Packers to be more aggressive when they got deep into Seattle territory.

"I think it's convenient to go for it now," McCarthy said. "But like I said, you have a game plan. You feel how you match up going into the game, was very confident with the defense going into it and just the way they started. That's where my confidence was."

The defense forced a three-and-out possession by the Seahawks and the Packers offense finally broke through. Rodgers connected with Cobb on a 13-yard touchdown pass, capping a seven-play, 56-yard drive. As the first quarter came to a close, the Packers had a 13–0 lead.

The Packers added a second-quarter field goal and led 16–0 at half-time. Green Bay's dominance was astounding! The Packers had 178 yards of offense against the top defense in football. Meanwhile, the Packers' defense held Seattle to just 59 yards, intercepted Wilson three times, and recovered a fumble.

In addition to forcing four fumbles, the Packers were physically whipping the Seahawks. But it was still only 16–0, and I wondered if those drives to the Seattle 1-yard line early in the game—resulting in field goals rather than touchdowns—would come back to haunt the Packers at some point.

The normally boisterous CenturyLink Field crowd was silenced. But that was soon to change.

The Packers still led 16–0 with less than five minutes left in the third quarter when the Seahawks lined up for a 37-yard field goal. Seattle punter Jon Ryan, a onetime Packer, was the holder on the play, and took off to the left.

Ryan was supposed to run for the first down. But when Ryan saw linebacker A.J. Hawk approach, he lofted a 19-yard touchdown pass to offensive lineman Gary Gilliam—a former tight end—that pulled the Seahawks within 16–7.

"Well, I mean, fakes are risky," McCarthy said. "And Jon Ryan can run, we know that. I think from the responsibility standpoint, pursuit and so forth, I think it would've been a foot race for the first down. We did not execute our particular responsibilities as best we can, and they had a better play call than what we had called."

The Packers extended their lead to 19–7 on a 48-yard Crosby field goal with just less than 11 minutes remaining.

After both teams punted, Seattle began at its own 46-yard line. But Wilson's pass to Jermaine Kearse was intercepted by Morgan Burnett.

The Packers safety had a world of space in front of him, but at the urging of teammate Julius Peppers, fell to the ground at the Green Bay 43. Instead of potentially having possession deep in Seattle territory, the Packers started a drive at their own 43-yard line with 5:04 to go in the game.

"It was late in the game when I caught it," Burnett said. "I saw Julius Peppers look at me and give me the 'no mas' signal. That means get down. We were just more so concerned about securing the possession of the ball, getting our offense back on the field for another possession.

225

"I don't take nothing back that I did. It's easy to sit here after it happens to sit here and say you should've done this or should've done that."

I didn't think much of it at the time. I saw Burnett go down and I thought he was just trying to secure the ball for the offense. Still, leading by two scores with just more than five minutes to go, I felt the offense would run out the clock as they had the week before against Dallas.

In the booth, for the first time, I was starting to think, *Maybe the Packers have this!*

But the Packers weren't facing a depleted Dallas defense. This was the best defense in football across the line and they knew what was coming next.

Three ill-fated Eddie Lacy running plays lost a total of four yards. Tim Masthay came on to punt, and the Packers weren't out of the woods yet.

With 3:52 to go in the game, the Seahawks still had not scored against Green Bay's defense. Seattle's began at its own 31-yard line, and with Wilson suffering through the worst day of his professional career, it was Beast Mode time!

Lynch, the Seahawks' mercurial running back, started the drive with a 14-yard run. Wilson went to the air for 20 yards to Baldwin and then, following an incompletion, Wilson hit Lynch on what appeared to be a 35-yard touchdown. Replays ruled that Lynch did not come down with both feet in bounds, though, and the play was reversed.

Wilson came right back to Lynch on a 26-yard pass play to the Green Bay 9-yard line. Lynch then rushed for four yards up the middle to the Packers' 5-yard line. With 2:36 remaining, Wilson had a four-yard run, then he scored on the following play.

Green Bay's lead was now 19–14 with 2:09 remaining.

The game then turned from strange to absurd. Seattle executed an onside kick and the ball bounced high into the air, right at Packers tight end Brandon Bostick.

Bostick tried to make a play on the ball, but it went right through his hands. Seattle's Chris Matthews recovered at the 50-yard line.

Bostick's job was to block on the play and let wideout Jordy Nelson make the catch. When the ball bounced right at Bostick, he could not help himself. Instead of just doing his job and relying on his teammate to do his, Bostick tried to do too much.

"I guess I just reacted to it," Bostick said. "I just saw the ball and went to get the ball, which wasn't my job. That's all I can say about that. I'm human. I made a mistake."

The Packers still led 19–14 with just 2:07 to go. But the Seahawks had all of the momentum.

Wilson rushed for 15 yards to start the Seattle drive. Lynch then gained a yard on a run at the two-minute warning.

Wilson then hit tight end Luke Wilson for eight yards to the Green Bay 24. On the next play, Lynch was in full Beast Mode and rumbled 24 yards for a touchdown, giving Seattle its first lead of the night at 20–19.

Seahawks coach Pete Carroll called for the two-point conversion and Wilson was flushed to his right, then back to his left. Wilson finally lobbed a pass in the general direction of tight end Luke Wilson. Clinton-Dix misplayed the ball and Luke Wilson hauled in the pass to give Seattle a 22–19 lead.

"For the majority of the game, we were playing really good as a team," safety Morgan Burnett said. "Just the last couple minutes at the end changed it. That's football.

"You have to play to the very end. You never know what could happen."

In my opinion, this is where the greatness of Aaron Rodgers came to the forefront. Trailing by three, facing the top defense in the NFL, Rodgers got the ball with 1.25 to go.

Rodgers marshaled his team from the Green Bay 22 to the Seattle 30-yard line in six plays. Rodgers found Nelson for 15 yards to start the drive. He hit Cobb for 15 more. Rodgers scrambled on that bad calf for 12 yards to the Seahawks 36. And after two incompletions, he hit Nelson for six yards on third down.

With 19 seconds to go, Crosby came on and drilled one of the most important, clutch field goals of his career. Through a swirling wind, Crosby hammered a "no doubt about it" 48-yard game-tying field goal, and the NFC Championship Game was headed to overtime tied at 22.

I think all of us watching that game—media, fans, and players—were numb by the time overtime began. Seattle won the toss and Russell Wilson showed his resilience.

Five times in the game, Wilson had thrown to Jermaine Kearse. Four times, he was intercepted.

On the sixth play of overtime, on his sixth throw of the day to Kearse, Wilson looped a 35-yard rainbow dropped right over the top of cornerback Tramon Williams, who gave up inside position on the play.

The Packers blitzed on the play, leaving Williams with no safety help. And when Kearse hauled in the perfect throw from Wilson for a 35-yard touchdown, Seattle had an improbable 28–22 victory.

Why improbable?

Well, Green Bay held a 16–0 halftime lead. And according to ProFootballReference.com, the Packers' chances of winning at that point were 94.4 percent.

Green Bay also led 19–7 with just more than three minutes left in the game. And at that moment, the Packers' chances of winning were 99.9 percent.

"I tried to watch the film...but I didn't," Packers left guard Josh Sitton said. "I couldn't watch it. I knew what happened. We kicked their ass up front, and the whole game. We handled them all day. We should've won the game."

Back in the 2003 divisional playoffs, the Philadelphia Eagles converted a fourth-and-26 play in the final minute of regulation, and went on to defeat the Packers 20–17 in overtime. Two professors from the University of Wisconsin–Green Bay later calculated that the Eagles' chances of converting that play were 1-in-87, or 1.15 percent.

Amazingly, the Seahawks had poorer odds during several points of the 2014 NFC title game.

"It's a missed opportunity that I will probably think about the rest of my career," Rodgers said. "We were the better team…and we played well enough to win and we can't blame anybody but ourselves."

I left with many varied opinions after that game. Like everyone else, I was numb. I felt so bad for the Packers, who had really come together as the 2014 season evolved. It took a while, but by the end of the season, for the first time since 2010, the Packers truly had a Super Bowl–caliber team. Unfortunately, they did not get to the big game.

Even to this day, it is still hard to reflect on the missed opportunity that day because I feel so bad for that great group of people. The brilliance of Rodgers and his receivers, the power of Eddie Lacy, the might of a healthy offensive line, and the improvement of the defense in the second half of the season were testament to great coaching, talented players, and a drive and determination of a special group.

I felt terrible for the great outside linebacker Julius Peppers. After being cut by Chicago, he signed with Green Bay because he felt the Packers gave him the best chance to get to and win a Super Bowl. At 35 years old, Peppers delivered an All-Pro season with seven sacks, two interceptions returned for touchdowns, six forced fumbles, and three fumble recoveries.

Peppers' impact within the walls of the locker room was so profound that his teammates elected him a captain for the postseason. That rarely, if ever, happens with a new player on an established team. Quite frankly, Peppers was the Packers' best defensive player in that postseason. He made 11 tackles, 2.5 sacks, and forced two fumbles, including a crucial one against Dallas in the Divisional Round of the playoffs.

I know this is not popular to say among Packers fans, but what a performance in the final four minutes of that game and in overtime by Seattle quarterback Russell Wilson. In the middle of the worst nightmare of his professional career, he rallied that team, and down the stretch made one play after another. His performance in the face of that adversity was impressive.

Yes, the Packers certainly did their part to help Wilson, but his "about-face" performance late in the fourth quarter of a game that was all but lost was impressive.

Two weeks later, the Seahawks suffered a tremendous loss of their own. They were at the New England goal line in the final seconds of the Super Bowl. Instead of handing the football to All-Pro running back Marshawn Lynch and letting him run it in from the 1-yard line for the game-winning score, the Seahawks called a passing play.

New England cornerback Malcolm Butler stepped in front of the pass and made a game-saving interception, and the Patriots prevailed 28–24. The Patriots—a team Green Bay had defeated two months earlier—won their fourth Super Bowl since 2001 and denied the Seahawks a second consecutive Lombardi trophy.

There were consequences following the Seattle game, as well.

In 2015, the Packers brought back just about all of their key players, giving them an opportunity to finish the job that had slipped away in the final four minutes at Seattle. But I believe there is a residual impact to a devastating loss like the Packers experienced in the NFC Championship Game. There is an impact on the psyche of a team.

By the time the Seahawks and Packers met in Week 2 of the 2015 season, it was quite apparent neither team was anywhere close to being as good as they were that winter day in Seattle.

In my preparation for that game, I finally went back and watched the television copy of the NFC Championship Game for the first time. Almost eight months later, the perspective I gained was enlightening.

I knew the Packers had dominated most of that game. After all, I was there. But I didn't realize how dominant they were that day. The Packers were truly the better team. The fact they didn't win the game was akin to missing the opportunity of a lifetime.

I couldn't help but think you just don't walk away from a loss like the Packers experienced in the NFC Championship Game like it never happened.

Jordy Nelson was injured in the 2015 preseason, a crippling blow for those Packers. But that wasn't the whole story.

The burden Green Bay carried from that day in Seattle weighed on it like a ball and chain. The locker-room feel was different from 2014.

The offense sputtered all season, and the frustration was palpable. The defense was solid, but wasn't championship caliber.

Special teams were much improved under new coordinator Ron Zook, who took over when Shawn Slocum was fired after his unit was a major reason the Packers lost in Seattle.

The 2015 Packers fought the good fight. They lost the division title in a bitter defeat at the hands of Minnesota at Lambeau Field on the final day of the regular season. They rallied in the playoffs to beat Washington, then fell in an epic game at Arizona.

The Seahawks struggled for most of the 2015 season, as well. Like the Packers, they relinquished their division title, won a wild-card game at Minnesota when the Vikings missed a chip-shot field goal to win, and then fell at Carolina to the eventual NFC Champion Panthers.

We are all products of our experiences, and the experiences the Packers and Seahawks went through at the end of the playoffs following the 2014 season had a major impact on their psyche the following year.

They just weren't the same. How could they be?

Getting to the Super Bowl and winning it is hard enough. Staying on top in today's NFL might be even more difficult.

The system does not lend itself to sustained success by any single team. In the past seven years, New England and Green Bay are the only teams to defy the odds and the system by making the playoffs each year.

Twelve teams make the playoffs each season, six from each conference. Barring a trade, those teams draft from No. 21 to No. 32 in each round. The system has the league's worst teams picking at the top of each round and the top teams drafting at the bottom. Barring a surprise, you just don't get the same caliber of player when you pick at the bottom of every round as the teams drafting near the top.

There is a "hard" salary cap in the NFL, and as the 2016 season began, that cap was at $155.27 million. Free agency plus the salary cap works against successful teams. It makes it tough to keep all of the good players a winning organization has developed because the salary cap restriction won't allow it.

For example, the "draft and develop" Packers have 63.8 percent of their salary cap going to 11 players in 2016 per Spotrac. That group includes Aaron Rodgers, Clay Matthews, Sam Shields, Julius Peppers, Randall Cobb, Jordy Nelson, Mike Daniels, Josh Sitton, T.J. Lang, Morgan Burnett, and Bryan Bulaga. Of those, Peppers is the only player that wasn't drafted and developed by Green Bay.

After the 2016 season, offensive linemen David Bakhtiari, Lang, and Sitton, along with Eddie Lacy, Peppers, Datone Jones, Micah Hyde, Sam Barrington, Nick Perry, Jared Cook, and J.C. Tretter, will be eligible for free agency. When this book went to press, the Packers had just $9 million in salary cap space.

The system does not give teams a break even if they do try "doing it right" by drafting, developing, and paying their own. Eventually, the salary cap squeezes good players off of good teams because you can't pay everyone.

So how do you keep the Super Bowl window open? It takes a great organization with stability in the front office, from ownership to general manager to head coach. It doesn't hurt to have a Hall-of-Fame-caliber quarterback. The Packers and Patriots have these elements in place, and that's why they have been able to sustain success despite the system being stacked against them.

The Packers' run behind quarterbacks Brett Favre and Aaron

Rodgers has included 19 playoff berths, six NFC Championship Game appearances, three trips to the Super Bowl, and two Super Bowl wins since 1992. That kind of sustained success in this day and age is rare.

Going forward, the Packers' challenge is an awesome one. Green Bay must keep the window open as it evolves from the group of players that won Super Bowl XLV to the next generation of champions.

EPILOGUE

Back in the late 1980s, while I was broadcasting Chicago Bears football on WGN radio, I was driving into Green Bay with our two analysts, Dick Butkus, the Hall of Fame linebacker of the Bears, and Hub Arkush, the publisher and editor of *Pro Football Weekly*.

We were driving past Lambeau Field and talking about the football experience in Green Bay. Now, mind you, the Packers were in the throes of decades of losing since the glory days of Lombardi.

Butkus remarked to us, "I could have played here." Both Arkush and I looked at each other incredulously. The quintessential Bear saying he could have played for the Packers?

Butkus went on to say, "I would have had no trouble playing here." It wasn't that he was a closet Packers fan. Nothing could be further from the truth. It wasn't that he regretted playing for his hometown team; rather, he embraced it. I believe he appreciated Green Bay, the place, for what it was for a football player—even during the losing years.

Butkus was no-nonsense, blood-and-guts, meat-and-potatoes—pure football. When he played the game, he had a singularity of purpose and focus—two things that come with being a football player in Green Bay.

The fan in me was visualizing a linebacking corps of Hall of Famers—Butkus, Ray Nitschke, and Dave Robinson—on the field for coach Vince Lombardi in the late 60s.

Somewhat along that train of thought, Lombardi himself once remarked, "You have a better chance for sustained success in a smaller town, without the distractions of the big city." Lombardi was from New York. He knew the distractions of the big city.

In this electronic world of satellite radio and TV, market size doesn't matter the way it did 30 years ago. The Internet, social media, Twitter, and Facebook have changed the way news travels. Everything is capable of being national and anyone's tweet can go viral in an instant.

From a marketing standpoint, a player doesn't have to be in New York, Chicago, or Los Angeles to have a national imprint. We've talked about how the Packers have been a national team since the 1960s. About how Green Bay rejuvenated its national appeal with Brett Favre and Reggie White in the 1990s.

Today the NFL shield and everyone under it are national. If the Packers win, they become a national story. Aaron Rodgers and Clay Matthews are prime examples of national commercial opportunities available for players in Green Bay, as much as they are for players from bigger towns.

From a football standpoint, Lambeau Field is the historic football cathedral of the NFL. The football facilities are the best in the league. No organization treats its players, even the alumni players, better than the Packers. And as Lombardi found more than a half century ago, without many distractions, sustained success is easier to attain in a smaller town.

Free agency wasn't supposed to be kind to the small markets in the NFL. But the Packers are the second-winningest organization in pro football since unfettered free agency came to the fore in 1993. New England leads the way with a 246–122–0 record, while the Packers are 235–132–1. Both franchises also have 17 playoff appearances in that time.

Following the retirement of Bob Harlan at the end of the 2008 campaign, the Packers Executive Committee Board of Directors made a wise choice in selecting Northwestern University athletic director Mark Murphy as the club's CEO.

Murphy brought a diverse background to the top administration job. He was an All-Pro safety on coach Joe Gibbs' Super Bowl XVII championship team in Washington. Murphy earned his MBA from American University's Kogod School of Business, graduated with a law degree from Georgetown University, and was the Redskins' representative to the NFLPA. He went on to become the athletic director at his alma mater, Colgate University, then Northwestern, and is now the chief executive of the Packers.

Murphy is highly regarded at 345 Park Avenue in New York—NFL Headquarters—because of his skill and talent in all phases of the business. His vast experience as a player in the league, a union official, and of course, an administrator of an NFL team makes him uniquely qualified to run the Packers and gives him impact at the league level.

Murphy has overseen the growth of the Packers organization to nearly twice the size of the company he came to in late 2008. No longer is it a little organization at 1265 Lombardi Avenue operating out of a pillbox building at the end of the north end zone at Lambeau Field. The one where in 1999 I could walk into the front door and proceed up a flight of stairs and right into the office of the CEO to shoot the breeze for a few minutes. Today this is a big company, in a big building, doing big things. There is nothing little about the Green Bay Packers.

Like Harlan before him, Murphy is an outstanding people person. He is a skilled orator who connects freely in public settings with media and fans across the country. He will take any question and give an answer that not only enlightens, but also respects the question and the person asking it.

The nearly seamless transition from Bob Harlan, one of the most beloved, respected, and personable figures in the history of the Green Bay Packers, to Mark Murphy is a testament to Murphy himself.

The formula for success in Green Bay is very simple. The business operation provides the football team with the resources to win. There are no family members in the ownership group waiting for a yearly financial stipend from the team or shareholders looking for a return on their investment.

Oh, make no mistake—the Packers have shareholders! Presently, 360,760 people own shares of stock in the Green Bay Packers. One of them is the president of the United States, Barack Obama. But not one Packers shareholder gets any financial return on his or her investment. Nor does he or she expect one.

In the summer of 2011, at the White House recognition of the Packers' Super Bowl XLV championship, the team presented the President with one share of stock in the Green Bay Packers. The President, a longtime Chicago Bears fan, immediately proposed a trade of Aaron Rodgers to his beloved Bears. It was Charles Woodson who put the kibosh on the proposed deal this way: "Remember, Mr. President, you're a minority owner." Aren't we all?!

The Packers put every dime of return on investment back into the football operation.

In a quarterback-driven business, many will tell you the Packers are fortunate to have had Brett Favre and Aaron Rodgers back-to-back. This is the most successful quarterback tandem since Joe Montana and Steve Young played consecutively in San Francisco in the 1980s and 1990s. This type of occurrence doesn't just happen. It is a product of good management. People who have a vision and the conviction to follow that vision often appear to be fortunate.

General manager Ron Wolf followed his instincts and acquired Favre for a first-round draft pick after Favre had been taken by the Falcons with a second-round selection in the previous draft.

By the same token, Rodgers fell to Ted Thompson in the draft. But Thompson stayed with his draft board, which told him Rodgers was the best player left when it was the Packers' turn to make a selection in the first round of the 2005 draft. So with the 24th pick, Thompson selected the quarterback when his team had more pressing needs at other positions that season.

With the current draft and-develop program that is in place, the Packers primarily have a homegrown team that has maintained good salary-cap health. That has been accomplished under the leadership of Ted Thompson and vice president of football administration/player finance Russ Ball. I can't remember the last time the Packers could not keep a player they really wanted due to salary-cap restrictions.

Ball's skill in this area is unquestioned. Thompson's discipline in free agency may frustrate some who would like to see the Packers be more active in that area. But his model has led to a team that can compete for the Super Bowl year after year.

Lambeau Field is a bucket-list destination along the lines of Fenway Park in Boston, Wrigley Field in Chicago, and Madison Square Garden in New York. It is unquestionably the most unique setting in the NFL. Visiting coaches and players look forward to playing in Green Bay, and the Packers have thrived there in the last quarter of a century.

Game day in Green Bay is still one of the most sought-after spectator experiences in pro sports.

The prologue of this book is titled "Why Green Bay?" In conclusion, I ask, "Why not Green Bay?!"

Made in the USA
Monee, IL
13 November 2023

46392709R00144